THE WAY
THEY PLAY

THE BLUES-ROCK MASTERS

by HP Newquist and Rich Maloof

Backbeat
Books

San Francisco

Published by Backbeat Books
600 Harrison Street, San Francisco, CA 94107
www.backbeatbooks.com
email: books@musicplayer.com
An imprint of the Music Player Group
Publishers of *Guitar Player*, *Bass Player*, *Keyboard*, and other magazines
United Entertainment Media, Inc.
A CMP Information company

CMP
United Business Media

Distributed to the book trade in the US and Canada by
Publishers Group West, 1700 Fourth Street, Berkeley, CA 94710

Distributed to the music trade in the US and Canada by
Hal Leonard Publishing, P.O. Box 13819, Milwaukee, WI 53213

Cover Design: Richard Leeds - bigwigdesign.com
Cover Photo: Ken Settle
Design: Richard Leeds - bigwigdesign.com

Library of Congress Cataloging-in-Publication Data

Newquist, H.P. (Harvey P.)
    The blues-rock masters / by HP Newquist and Richard Maloof.
        p. cm – (The way they play)
    Includes discographies.
    Contents: The players – Buddy Guy – Eric Clapton – Jimi Hendrix –
Jimmy Page – Duane Allman – Albert Collins – Roy Buchanan – Stevie Ray
Vaughan – Kenny Wayne Shepherd.
    ISBN 0-87930-735-8 (alk. paper)
    1. Guitar – Instruction and study. 2. Blues (Music) – Instruction and
study. 3. Rock music – Instruction and study. 4. Guitarists – Biography.
I. Maloof, Rich. II. Title. III. Series.

MT580 .N48 2002
787.87'166143–dc21

                                                        2002038356

Printed in the United States of America
02 03 04 05 06   5 4 3 2 1

CONTENTS

INTRODUCTION

The Way They Play—The Blues-Rock Masters was created so musicians could explore and experience blues-rock guitar styles. Most guitarists today know a little bit about the blues—at least enough to hold their own in a jam—and are reasonably comfortable with one or more styles of rock. But blues-rock is its own beast, a hybrid that is more than an electrified version of blues or an elementary style of rock. It incorporates pieces of both worlds: the emotion and forms of the blues coupled with the fiery aggression of rock 'n' roll.

The guitarists we've chosen here represent masters from across the blues-rock spectrum, some closer to one end than the other. Their work as blues-rockers defines the genre and also provides a historical look at how the music has evolved. Because, despite its roots in the simple chord progressions and unadorned style of the blues, blues-rock can be very demanding. This is true in part because the techniques and tone developed by the players profiled here set such a high bar for everyone else.

Playing great blues-rock guitar means going beyond simple riffing and chording. It's about mastering control, tone, melodic sense, and dynamic range. It's about being musically expressive without simply spilling emotion out all over the tune. It's about understanding a guitar's unique characteristics and making the most of them with vibrato, bends, pull-offs, volume swells, pickup selection, and glass slides. Such elements are crucial to playing with authority. Forget the stomp pedal and the effects rack; with blues-rock it's got to come straight from your hands, your guitar, and your amp.

Our intention is to offer a clear and complete picture of how these nine players do what they do best. Beyond presenting you with a blueprint for copying licks, we created this book to give you a blues-rock foundation on which to build. We're presuming that players who read this book and learn from its examples already have a basic knowledge of the instrument. Because of that, we haven't revisited fundamental lessons or defined terms we think you'll already be familiar with. Instead, we've included biographies, gear, discographies, setups, and characteristic techniques of the artists covered.

Players wishing to add some new styles and even some new tricks to their repertoire will find plenty of material in the pages that follow and on the accompanying CD. It is our hope that we can give guitarists a new perspective on the artists covered and provide valuable insight into the way they play.

—HP Newquist and Rich Maloof

NOTATIONAL SYMBOLS

The following symbols are used in *The Blues-Rock Masters* to notate fingerings, techniques, and effects commonly used in guitar music. Certain symbols are found in either the tablature or the standard notation only, not both. For clarity, consult both systems.

4🎵 : Left-hand fingering is designated by small Arabic numerals near note heads (1=first finger, 2=middle finger, 3=third finger, 4=little finger, t=thumb).

p🎵 : Right-hand fingering designated by letters (p=thumb, i=first finger, m=middle finger, a=third finger, c=little finger).

②🎵 : A circled number (1-6) indicates the string on which a note is to be played.

◼ : Pick downstroke.

∨ : Pick upstroke.

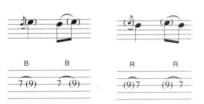

Bend: Play the first note and bend to the pitch of the equivalent fret position shown in parentheses.

Reverse Bend: Pre-bend the note to the specified pitch/fret position shown in parentheses. Play, then release to indicated pitch/fret.

Hammer-on: From lower to higher note(s). Individual notes may also be hammered.

Pull-off: From higher to lower note(s).

Slide: Play first note and slide up or down to the next pitch. If the notes are tied, pick only the first. If no tie is present, pick both.

A slide symbol before or after a single note indicates a slide to or from an undetermined pitch.

Finger vibrato.

Bar vibrato.

Bar dips, dives, and bends: Numerals and fractions indicate distance of bar bends in half-steps.

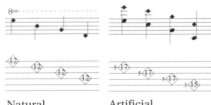

Natural harmonics.

Artificial harmonics.

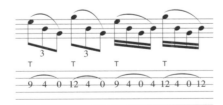

Pick-hand tapping: Notes are hammered with a pick-hand finger, usually followed by additional hammer-ons and pull-offs.

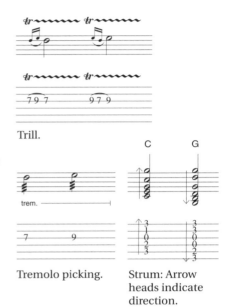

Trill.

Tremolo picking.

Strum: Arrow heads indicate direction.

HOW TABLATURE WORKS

The horizontal lines represent the guitar's strings, the top line standing for the high *E*. The numbers designate the frets to be played. For instance, a 2 positioned on the first line would mean play the 2nd fret on the first string (0 indicates an open string). Time values are indicated on the standard notation staff seen directly above the tablature. Special symbols and instructions appear between the standard and tablature staves.

CHORD DIAGRAMS

In all chord diagrams, vertical lines represent the strings, and horizontal lines represent the frets. The following symbols are used:

▬▬▬ Nut; indicates first position.

X Muted string, or string not played.

○ Open string.

⌒ Barre (partial or full).

● Placement of left-hand fingers.

‖‖ Roman numerals indicate the fret at which a chord is located.

Arabic numerals indicate left-hand fingering.

BLUES BASICS

BLUES FORMS

The most common form (musical structure) for blues-rock tunes is the 12-bar blues. While selections are not limited exclusively to this measure count and chord sequence, the blues is intimately connected with this structure. The phrases "playing a blues," "playing blues changes" or "playing a I–IV–V" all point to classic blues form.

There are two essential varieties of 12-bar blues.

The first type, shown here in the key of *E,* is simple and has few chord changes. Measures are shown in groups of four in accordance with how the form is felt and most easily memorized.

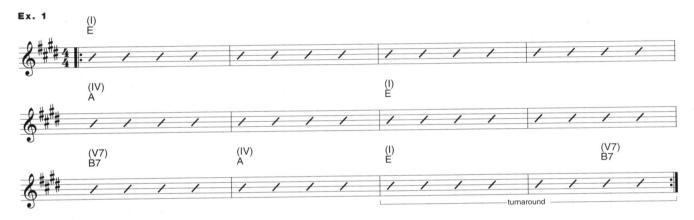

The second variety of 12-bar blues uses the same framework as the first but contains more-frequent chord changes. In **Ex. 2**, note where the changes feature chord tones other than the root in the bass (shown with slashes); these chords, called inversions, provide common tones between chords. Because there is more movement among the changes, the form has a feeling of more momentum, making it a popular choice for slower-tempo songs. This example incorporates the dominant 7 chord, a common substitution for the major triad, on each chord.

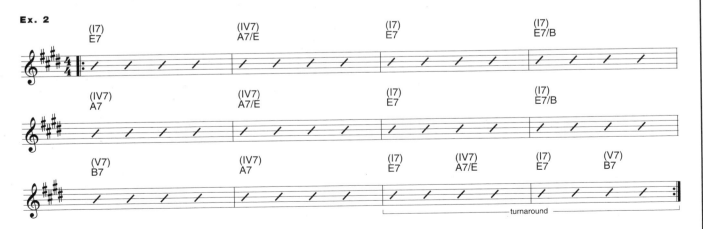

KEYS

A typical blues progression uses only three essential changes and is simple to transpose to any key. This chart shows the I, IV, and V chords—that is, the first (tonic), fourth (sub-dominant), and fifth (dominant) chords of a key—for the most common guitar-based blues.

KEY	I	IV	V7
E	E	A	B7
A	A	D	E7
B♭	B♭	E♭	F7
F	F	B♭	C7
G	G	C	D7
D	D	G	A7
C	C	F	G7

The V chord is always a dominant 7, and is shown here as such; in many instances you will hear the changes in a blues harmonized with additional chord tones (7, 9, ♭9, 11, 13. See **Chords** on the next page).

Once you become familiar with blues progressions and how they relate to positions on the guitar's neck, you will find it easy to transpose the changes by simply shifting position.

Note: In minor keys (e.g., an "*E* minor blues"), the I chord is always minor; the IV chord is usually minor but can be major or dominant; and the V chord remains a dominant 7.

THE BLUES SCALE

The blues scale is the foundation of blues-rock soloing. The vast majority of music examples in this book are derived from the notes of this scale.

Guitarists can improvise over a blues progression using the blues scale that carries the name of the key. For example, you can solo over the entire I–IV–V progression in *G* (*G–C–D7*) using only the notes in a *G* blues scale. Advanced players often change the blues scale they use to match the progression, emphasizing or "bringing out" the changes; in a *G* blues, they'll use a *G* scale over the I chord, a *C* scale over the IV, and a *D* scale over the V7. Note that the blues scale can be applied to both major and minor harmonies.

The blues scale is most closely related to the minor pentatonic scale, with one distinct difference: a ♭5 (flatted fifth) degree, the defining characteristic of a blues scale. This "blue note" provides a dissonance within its key and allows for a three-note chromatic climb from the 4th degree to the ♮5. See the scale degrees in **Ex. 3** to compare blues, minor pentatonic, and major scales in the key of *C*.

Ex. 3

C Blues

R   ♭3   4   ♭5   5   ♭7   (R)

C Minor Pentatonic

R   ♭3   4   5   ♭7   (R)

C Major

R   2   3   4   5   6   7   (R)

Ex. 4 shows a neck diagram of the classic blues scale, often referred to as "the blues box." This pattern works in any key; "R" shows the position of a given key's root note within the pattern. So to place the box in the key of *G*, you would start on the bottom string's 3rd fret.

Though some blues-rock players solo within the confines of the box, the notes of the blues scale can of course be found all over the guitar's neck. **Ex. 5** shows a neck diagram of the blues scale across a 12-fret range.

CHORDS

Ex. 6 shows a sampling of chord shapes commonly used in blues-rock. Chord shapes are shown in two varieties: with the root on the 6th string and with the root on the 5th. For example, an *F7* chord can be played with the root at the 1st fret (6th-string root) or the 8th fret (5th-string root).

Ex. 6

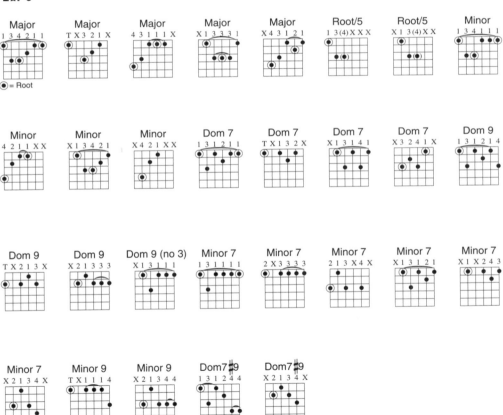

BLUES-ROCK
MASTERS

THE PLAYERS

CHAPTER 1 Buddy Guy

Buddy Guy is the man who forged the direct link between the blues and rock 'n' roll, creating the foundation of blues-rock guitar. Over the past 30 years, guitarists from Jimi Hendrix to Eric Clapton have said that much of their inspiration came from Guy, who melded blistering electric blues with explosive technique and showmanship to give shape to modern rock guitar. Guy remains a tasteful yet aggressive player who amps up the blues to a rocking good time, and he is perhaps the only guitar player still alive—and playing—who is blues-rock's direct link to its past.

BIOGRAPHY

George "Buddy" Guy was born on July 30, 1936, in Lettsworth, Louisiana. He picked cotton during most of his youth and would listen to records like John Lee Hooker's "Boogie Chillen" when he could afford them. As a teenager Guy taught himself guitar and eventually found work playing in small clubs around Baton Rouge. As his instrumental prowess grew, he decided his musical future was not to be found in the South. Barely 20 years old, he took a train to Chicago and played in any club that would have him.

As a way to win bar bets and guitar duels with established players such as Magic Sam and Otis Rush, Guy learned to wow the crowds with fingerboard flash and showmanship. He bought a 150-foot-long cord (an accessory first popularized by Magic Sam and also used by Albert Collins), which allowed him to walk through the audience—and right out of the bar—while playing his solos. Other blues guitarists, many of whom remained seated while performing, scratched their heads at what young Buddy was doing. But Guy never failed to drive the crowds wild.

Because nobody really knew what to make of his incendiary blues style, Guy's gigs were limited to late-night bar stints where the crowds were booze-fueled and brawling. Legend has it that by the time Muddy Waters saw him in a club in 1957, Guy was ready to quit the bar circuit and head back South. But Waters—the man credited with electrifying the blues—recognized Buddy's talent and became his mentor, getting him a job as session guitarist for Chess Records. There Guy backed such notables as Willie Dixon, Sonny Boy Williamson, and Howlin' Wolf. Buddy's versatile sound and style allowed him to perfectly complement each of these artists, and he ultimately became an excellent mimic of their styles.

As a sideman, though, he had to keep his playing toned down and restrained. These were straight blues records, after all, and Guy's wild persona was kept to a minimum to suit the mood. Live, though, he continued to play louder and more frenetically, hanging from low ceiling fixtures by his knees and playing his guitar behind his back and with his teeth. Onstage, Buddy Guy was creating the first blues-rock performances.

Guy released several singles produced by Willie Dixon, and in 1962 he recorded

"Stone Crazy," which went to No. 12 on the R&B charts. Yet it barely hinted at Guy's revolutionary style. Because Chess was a blues label, it missed the boat on Buddy's playing. Instead, a young Jimi Hendrix, who had seen Guy's wild stage show and heard his hard-edged blues—he was even caught taping a Guy performance—took the style to London. Hendrix incorporated elements of Guy's act into his own and soon became an international icon.

Just as Hendrix was breaking, Guy went to Vanguard Records and released albums such as *A Man and the Blues* and *This Is Buddy Guy*. He teamed up with harp player Junior Wells, and the two of them became a popular act known as the Blues Brothers during the late '60s and early '70s.

By this time, guitarists like Clapton and Hendrix were openly acknowledging Guy's influence. Clapton, who at the time was hailed as a guitar god in his own right, called Guy "the greatest guitarist alive." In an effort to create a blues-rock haven for himself and other guitarists, Buddy bought a Chicago club called the Checkerboard Lounge. Yet, for all the praise and recognition he was getting from other guitarists, the general public was ignoring him. His recording career waned and his club went out of business.

Buddy Guy all but disappeared from view during the era of hard rock and metal. He recorded only sporadically and played mostly small clubs throughout the '70s and into the '80s. Then, in 1989, he was invited to headline the Chicago Blues Festival as a testament to his affiliation with the city. After his performance, everyone seemed to remember just why he was so important and influential. Suddenly, everyone wanted to know about Buddy Guy. He took another stab at running his own blues club, opening Legends that same year. The club attracted blues-rock fans from all over the world who could now see Guy at his best—live, on his own stage.

Two years later, Guy was signed to Silvertone, his first record deal in more than a decade, and started releasing his brand of blues-rock on a national level. With guests ranging from Clapton and Jeff Beck to John Fogerty and Mark Knopfler, he released *Damn Right, I've Got the Blues* (which earned him a Grammy), *Slippin' In*, and *Feels Like Rain*.

After the release of these records, Guy's own legend was secure. He shared the stage with legions of guitarists who had learned from him, including Stevie Ray Vaughan, with whom Guy played on the night Vaughan died in a helicopter crash.

Guy has continued playing, and Legends has become a legendary hangout. Guy plays a number of dates there each year and hosts fellow guitar notables such as Clapton. True to form, Buddy Guy still uses that 150-foot cable, which audience members reverently hold above their heads as he makes his way to every corner of the room.

GEAR & SETUP

Buddy Guy has always favored Fender Stratocasters. He has no particular preferred guitar; he claims that as a traveling musician his guitars tend to get stolen. His most easily identifiable Strats are black with white polka dots, and he's been seen with similarly painted acoustics.

Guy plays with a very bright lead tone onstage, which he gets as a result of Lace Sensor pickups, Fender's TBX system (for passive tone control), a steel nut, and fresh strings. Guy uses especially thick fretwire, and his frets are set on top of the fingerboard finish, facilitating his enormous bends. Fender's Buddy Guy Stratocaster closely emulates his own guitar's setup. On occasion, Guy has been known to pick up a Gibson ES-335 or Les Paul.

CHECKLIST ✓

Guitar . . . . Fender Stratocaster

Neck . . . . Highly lacquered maple; soft V shape

Condition . . . Standard, often painted with polka dots

Setup . . . . Stock

Strings . . . . Custom-gauge Ernie Ball (.010, .012, .015, .028, .038, .048)

Pickups . . . . . . Three Lace Sensors; Fender TBX tone control

Pick . . . . Gibson, rounded triangle, light

Amp . . . . Fender Bassman, 4x10

Settings . . . . . BRIGHT channel, overdriven for lead

Effects . . . . Wah-wah pedal

Tone . . . . High midrange

Attack . . . . Strong, sometimes hamfisted

Signature traits . . . . Very wide bends; sporadic phrasing

Tricks . . . . Banging drumsticks on guitar's neck; playing with teeth; playing behind back; playing with guitar on floor

Influences . . . John Lee Hooker, B.B. King, Magic Sam, Muddy Waters, Guitar Slim, T-Bone Walker

Overall approach . . . . Loud and aggressive, showy

SELECTED DISCOGRAPHY

This Is Buddy Guy! (Vanguard, 1968)
Live in Montreux (Evidence, 1977)
Drinkin' TNT 'n' Smokin' Dynamite
  (Blind Pig, 1982)
Chess Masters (Chess, 1987)
Damn Right, I've Got the Blues
  (Silvertone, 1991)
The Very Best of Buddy Guy
  (Rhino, 1992)
The Complete Chess Studio Sessions
  (MCA/Chess, 1992)
Sweet Tea (Jive, 2001)
With Junior Wells:
Coming at You (Vanguard, 1968)
Play the Blues (Atlantic, 1972)
The Original Blues Brothers Live
  (Magnum, 1983)

RECOMMENDED CUTS

"Hold That Plane" (*The Very Best of
  Buddy Guy*)
"Five Long Years" (*The Very Best of
  Buddy Guy*)
"Blues at My Baby's House" (*The Very
  Best of Buddy Guy*)
"Ten Years Ago" (*The Very Best of
  Buddy Guy*)
"The First Time I Met the Blues" (*The
  Very Best of Buddy Guy*)
"Stone Crazy" (*The Very Best of
  Buddy Guy*)
"When You See the Tears from My
  Eyes" (*The Very Best of Buddy Guy*)
"There Is Something on Your Mind"
  (*Damn Right, I've Got the Blues*)
"Damn Right, I've Got The Blues"
  (*Damn Right, I've Got the Blues*)

Guy has used original and reissue tweed Fender Bassman amps since the 1950s, favoring its distinct BRIGHT channel. Unlike with his Strats, he's managed to keep specific amps for decades. He's recently reported to be enamored of the Fender Cyber-Twin for its ability to produce not only his tone but those of the artists he mimicked in his session days.

Little comes between Buddy Guy's guitar and amp aside from a Dunlop wah-wah, an occasional Boss octave pedal, and a 150-foot cable. Other than that, his tone is about as raw as it can get.

Early in his career, Guy's lead tone was bright and snappy. In later years, when he employed more overdrive (as on *Damn Right*), the distortion may have softened his amp tone a bit, but the bite of Guy's gritty attack was still audible. He took advantage of the available sustain, but you can still hear his distinctly heavy right hand strangling the strings.

STYLE & TECHNIQUE

You can hear the blues in every element of Buddy Guy's technique. As the successor to Muddy Waters, his playing and singing have come to define modern Chicago blues. The dynamic electric approach he brings to the blues pushes it into the realm of blues-rock.

Guy's sound is characterized by a strong pick attack, wide bends, and phrases that come in fitful bursts. He is so forceful and deliberate with his picking that he can sound heavy-handed, sometimes even rigid. He holds his pick (a rounded triangle) between his thumb and two fingers, which both reinforces the attack and enables him to palm the pick when he plucks with his fingers.

Like a baseball player warming up with two bats, Guy often practices on heavy-gauge strings and then performs with a lighter set. (Bending the life out of his strings requires that Guy keep a stack of spare *E*'s at the ready.) Blues players have always used bends to access the notes between half-steps, but few have stretched as far or as frequently as Guy. He almost always bends with his 3rd finger, supporting it with his 2nd or 1st fingers on higher bends or when he's on lower strings. He maintains good intonation even when he's pushing a note two-and-a-half steps above pitch.

Guy adds vibrato in the same style as B.B. King, either rapidly shaking or slowly rocking his left hand. This involves moving the entire hand from the wrist to the finger.

The phrasing of Guy's solos and fills is unpredictable, and he often enters on an unexpected beat or following a long breath of rests. At first, his improvised melodies come in short blasts, like someone formulating an argument. He often holds back until the turnaround before allowing the rest of his idea to tumble out to completion.

Guy generally stays in a key's home or "box" position (e.g., in an *A* blues, he's in either 5th or 12th position), though it's not uncommon for him to extend the position two frets to the north.

The Buddy Guy Lesson begins on page 20.

LESSON

Buddy Guy often punctuates his playing with quick flourishes that sound more verbal than guitaristic. In a short passage like **Ex. 1**, the timing is loose and upper-string passing tones blur together, resulting in a short phrase that sounds clipped and angry. Use your 3rd or 4th finger to catch the initial hit on high *C*. Then land in 8th position for the frenzied bit, which begins with a pull-off on the top string and resolves on a 3rd-string *E*. (*This brief lick is heard twice on the CD.*)

Ex. 1

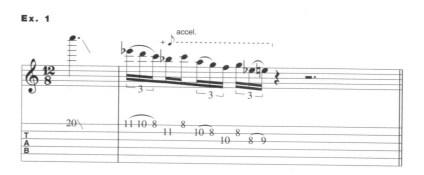

Good phrasing can be effective in filling a solo with tension and emotion. In **Ex. 2** tension builds with taut bends at the top of a I–IV–V. Pre-bend the high *B♭–E* double-stop so the pair descends a quarter-step as you enter the third phrase. Watch your intonation on the closing bend: It stretches up a whole step, releases to pitch, and then goes back up a half-step where the IV chord would come in.

Ex. 2

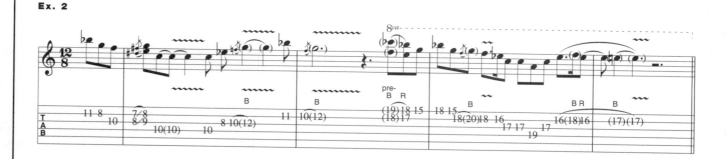

A strong bending finger is essential for imitating the Buddy Guy sound. Guy almost always uses his third finger to bend, even when he's catching other notes simultaneously. In the trademark move in **Ex. 3**, the 1st-string *C* (4th finger) stays put while the 3rd-string *D* (3rd finger) repeatedly bends up a whole-step to *E*. Notice that the 1st finger of your fretting hand naturally lays over the 5th fret; let it damp the 2nd string but not play an actual note (see the "X" notation in the tablature). This way you can strike all three top strings with your picking hand and still play only the notes shown.

Ex. 3

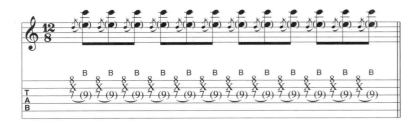

Guy occasionally uses a low-key solo entrance to set up contrast with the busier, more tense lines to come. Use a light hammer on **Ex. 4**'s opening *A* note, and roll quickly over the half-step ornaments on the 3rd string. Slide into the double-stops in the last bar from one fret below.

Ex. 4

CHAPTER 2 Eric Clapton

At the dawn of the blues-rock movement, there was one person who got everybody's attention and held it: Eric Clapton. No other guitarist took the blues and electrified it into something as unique and thrilling as Clapton did. Every player to follow EC would be compared to him.

More than many of the players in this book, Clapton was, and is, a blues purist—he has spent the majority of his career attempting to capture the spirit of the blues through the electric guitar. He helped turn the blues into hard rock—becoming a guitar icon in the process—and then gave up electricity for the simplicity of the acoustic guitar. In many ways, his career has been one long search for the devil at the crossroads.

BIOGRAPHY

Eric Patrick Clapp was born on March 30, 1945, in Ripley, Surrey, England. From the first, his life's course was like a road map of blues despair: a truly dysfunctional family, problems with drink and drugs, personal crises, and deaths of friends and relatives. All of these events would bind him closer to the music he would come to define.

After falling in love with Muddy Waters's sound, 14-year-old Clapton (using his mother's maiden name) picked up the guitar his grandparents had given him and immersed himself in the instrument. Dropping out of school, he played in second-tier bands like the Roosters and Casey Jones & the Engineers before he was asked to join the Yardbirds in 1963. The band soon gathered a following in London at the Crawdaddy Club, where audiences gave him the ironic nickname "Slowhand." Playing a Fender Telecaster through a Vox AC30, Clapton delivered sparse and raw electric blues.

Signed to Epic, the Yardbirds produced commercially oriented fare that increasingly stuck in Clapton's craw. Disgusted with the band's direction, he quit in 1965, in the middle of tracking "For Your Love." He disappeared for a few months, spending the time improving his blues chops in a self-imposed solitary confinement.

When he was ready to return to performing, Clapton joined John Mayall's Bluesbreakers. Mayall was England's godfather of the blues, and in the midst of the UK blues explosion, any blues player of note—from vocalists and guitarists to bassists and drummers—passed through his band.

With Clapton, Mayall's Bluesbreakers became transcendent—the ultimate blues-based jam band. There were no pop or commercial aspirations, no pyschedelia. And Clapton became, as the graffiti of the time noted, "God." Mayall let Eric indulge his blues obsession to the fullest, and Clapton took advantage of the opportunity, incorporating electrified Texas and Chicago blues styles into his playing. His solos got longer, more confident, and more energetic as the cheering crowds grew.

This Bluesbreakers line-up recorded one album, *Bluesbreakers with Eric Clapton*, which showcased Clapton's abilities as a player who could hammer out the blues with a rock sensibility. But Clapton again felt he needed a new venue in which to explore the blues, and he had left the band by the time the album was released. Numerous session dates followed. Clapton recorded with blues heroes Otis Spann and Muddy Waters, and he made his first recording of Robert Johnson's "Crossroads" with a pickup band called Powerhouse.

Another Powerhouse member was bassist/vocalist Jack Bruce. Teaming with Bruce and drummer Ginger Baker, Clapton found the outlet he'd been looking for. This time it was blues-rock—a searing manifestation of the electric blues—in the supertrio Cream. With a heavy rhythm-section sound applied to music based on blues conventions, Cream contributed as much as any previous band or artist to the establishment of blues-rock and hard rock.

With its first release, *Fresh Cream*, in 1967, Cream sent blues-rock into overdrive. Clapton's solos on classic blues numbers like Willie Dixon's "Spoonful" took everything he'd done with his previous bands and pushed it as far as it could go. Through it all, Clapton played a Gibson SG–style Les Paul running through 100-watt Marshall amps, creating the hard-rock prototype that endured for the rest of the century.

Clapton disbanded Cream after two years and formed Blind Faith. The supergroup was everything Cream had not been, with fewer jams and more emphasis on songs as well as Clapton's vocals and songwriting. Rounding out the rest of his musical repertoire, Clapton put his reverent blues playing on hiatus.

When Blind Faith disbanded after one album, Clapton seemed adrift. He signed on as a sideman with John Lennon, Delaney & Bonnie, George Harrison, and others, and finally settled down to try his hand as a solo artist. He released *Eric Clapton*, which featured "Blues Power" and "After Midnight," but these largely commercial songs had little to do with Clapton as a blues-rocker. Even his next step—recording with Duane Allman as part of Derek & the Dominos in 1970—was more rock- and pop-oriented. This period saw one Clapton blues-rock milestone, however, when he abandoned his Gibson/Marshall setup and began playing a Fender Stratocaster.

Two years of silence followed, marked by a descent into substance abuse. It took Pete Townshend and his *Eric Clapton at the Rainbow* concert to begin to bring Clapton out of his addiction and seclusion. In 1974 Clapton released *461 Ocean Avenue*, the first of several albums, including 1977's *Slowhand*, that set the tone for the guitarist's future solo albums: short songs, Clapton's vocals, sparse guitar, and mainstream appeal. Guitar purists wondered what had happened to the electrifying solos, but Clapton appeared comfortable experimenting with pop music for the next two decades, from film scores to radio-oriented albums.

It wasn't until his 1992 performance on MTV's *Unplugged* that Clapton chucked all of these explorations and returned to the blues. His next albums, beginning with 1994's *From the Cradle*, were pure blues and blues-rock concoctions. His live shows featured a reworking of many of his classic songs in a blues vein (to the dismay of his mainstream fans), yet Clapton finally seemed to have found a skin within which he was perfectly comfortable.

GEAR & SETUP

Eric Clapton sheds gear and styles like a snake shedding its skin. In the Yardbirds years he played a Fender Telecaster through a Vox AC30 amp. By 1966, in John

CHECKLIST ✓

Guitar . . . . Fender Stratocaster

Neck . . . . Maple

Condition . . . Mix and match

Setup . . . . ⅛" action the entire length of the neck

Strings . . . . Light: .009, .011, .016, .024, .032, .042 (occasionally one gauge higher, starting with .010s)

Pickups . . . . . . Vintage Noiseless with midboost and TBX circuit

Amp . . . . Marshalls, tweed Fenders

Settings . . . . . High volume, slightly overdriven

Effects . . . . Vox wah-wah

Tone . . . . Throaty for rhythm, crisp for leads

Picking . . . . . . Heavy-gauge pick held between thumb and index finger

Signature traits . . . . Long solo passages, lots of pull-offs, strong vibrato

Tricks . . . . Very few

Influences . . . Robert Johnson, Otis Rush, Buddy Guy, Howlin' Wolf, Chuck Berry, Muddy Waters, Freddie King, B.B. King, Albert King, Duane Eddy, Blind Willie Johnson

Overall approach . . . . Reverent, controlled, every note in its place

SELECTED DISCOGRAPHY

With the Yardbirds:
Five Live Yardbirds (Rhino, 1964)
With John Mayall:
Bluesbreakers with Eric Clapton
    (Deram, 1966)
With Howlin' Wolf:
The London Howlin' Wolf Sessions
    (Chess, 1971)
With Buddy Guy & Junior Wells:
Play the Blues (Atlantic, 1972)
With Cream:
The Very Best of Cream (Polydor, 1995)
Eric Clapton releases:
Slowhand (Polydor, 1977)
Crossroads (Polydor, 1988),
24 Nights (Reprise, 1991)
Unplugged (Atlantic, 1992)
From the Cradle (Reprise, 1994)

RECOMMENDED CUTS

"Crossroads" (*The Very Best of Cream*)
"Spoonful" (*The Very Best of Cream*)
"White Room" (*The Very Best of Cream*)
"Hideaway" (*Crossroads*)
"Good Morning Little Schoolgirl"
    (*Crossroads*)
"Peaches and Diesel" (*Slowhand*)
"Layla" (*Unplugged*)
"Before You Accuse Me" (*Journeyman*,
    Reprise, 1989)
"Forever Man" (*Behind the Sun*, Warner
    Bros., 1985)
"Motherless Children" (*461 Ocean
    Boulevard*, RSO, 1974)
*Many of these tracks also appear on
    various Clapton anthologies and
    "best of" collections*

Mayall's band, he was using the venerated Gibson Les Paul/Marshall setup, which he employed throughout most of Cream's existence. In the post-Cream years his diverse musical pursuits found him trying out a variety of instruments, including a custom Telecaster, the semi-hollow Gibson ES-335, and various Gibson Firebirds.

Surprisingly, the guitar that brought Clapton fame was a 1960 Les Paul Standard, which he played through an overdriven 45-watt Marshall 2x12 combo. He later used a 1961 Gibson SG–style Les Paul (known as the "psychedelic guitar" for its colorful paint job) through 100-watt Marshall heads and 4x12 cabinets. This latter combination went on to become a staple of rock guitarists for decades. For effects, Clapton used a Vox wah-wah and occasionally a Dallas-Arbiter Fuzz Face.

But this is not the gear we most commonly associate with Clapton—we think of him as a Strat master. Clapton switched to the Stratocaster nearly full time around the *Layla* sessions and used it almost exclusively over the next three decades. He built his famous Blackie model from a set of Strats he purchased in Nashville in 1970, creating it from parts of various guitars. He now plays an Eric Clapton Strat that uses three Vintage Noiseless pickups (formerly Lace Sensors), along with unique mid-boost circuitry. This guitar is modeled after the Blackie Strat.

Clapton constantly adjusts his pots live. He likes his fretwire fatter than a typical Strat's. He's been a proponent of tweed Fender Champ amps for his blues work, which also encompasses the acoustic. For the fabled *Unplugged* show, he played a 1939 Martin 000-42, and he also uses a 000-28. Martin has produced signature-edition versions of both models.

STYLE & TECHNIQUE

Clapton has almost always played in a gentlemanly manner. His style, then as now, is refined, almost as if concentration were just as important as emotion. Even his most scorching solos, such as on "Crossroads," have a sense of preparation rarely found in blues-rock. Clapton, unlike Stevie Ray Vaughan or Roy Buchanan, has rarely pushed his playing to the point where you thought he might just lose it. He is an aggressive guitarist, but a studied and thoughtful one. In rhythm parts as well as in leads, Clapton's performance is always controlled and measured. Every note counts.

He's also a fine mimic who does spot-on imitations of Muddy Waters, Freddie King, Albert King, and others, especially when covering their songs.

One of the most notable aspects of Clapton's style is his legendary "woman tone." Developed during his Cream days, this throaty sound is a combination of things. The guitar's tone knobs have to be set to zero, while the volume is all the way up. It helps to have the pickup switch in the neck position. Clapton uses light-gauge Ernie Ball Slinky strings, and he keeps his amps cranked. It also helps to use a wah-wah pedal rolled off from full to the choke mode—about halfway.

Clapton uses a heavy pick. He prefers to play his chords in lower and open positions, limiting his use of barre chords due to upper-neck intonation considerations. He rarely changes strings unless they break.

LESSON

Eric Clapton spent his developmental years emulating heroes like Elmore James, Muddy Waters, Buddy Guy, and Freddie King. He wrapped his predecessors' licks in warm distortion and reverb, but the lineage was always clear. A part like the one in **Ex. 1**, most likely to be played by Clapton in a rock setting, is straight out of the blues. This swinging lick features a cutting one-and-a-half-step bend on the top string.

Ex. 1

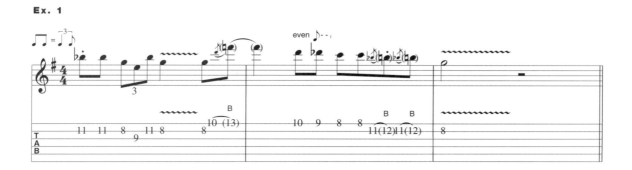

Consider **Ex. 2** vis-à-vis the previous lick to see how Clapton projected increasingly more rock elements onto his blues background as his career progressed. This prototypical blues-rock riff is played entirely within the *E* blues scale in 12th position.

Ex. 2

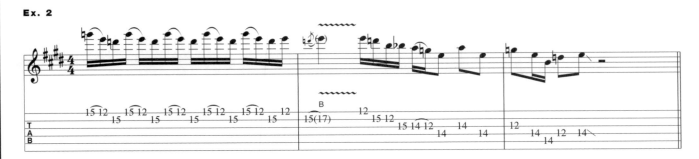

Though Clapton seldom interrupts his signal chain with effects, he has achieved great results with the occasional use of the wah pedal. The so-called psychedelic era found him taking cues from contemporaries like Jimi Hendrix while still carving out a path of his own. In **Ex. 3**'s fill, the wah pedal is fully depressed on the downbeats and in "up" position on the upbeats; simply rock your foot on the pedal as if you're keeping tempo. Clapton played this *C* blues lick with little ornamentation outside of the quick pull-off on beat *three* from the ♭5 (*G♭*) to the 4 (*F*).

Ex. 3

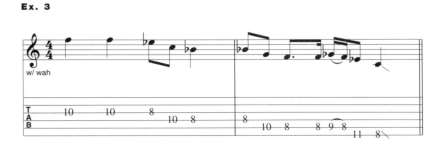

Clapton has long favored melancholy strains, and he's as much at home playing a ballad as an up-tempo rock tune. **Ex. 4** is characteristic of his approach to leads within ballads, where a plaintive melodic line develops from a few carefully chosen, well-articulated notes. Coming off of a high *F*, the introductory phrase sets the stage for something both bluesy and sweet. The gentle hammer-on and a quick slide in bar 2 add warmth and expression. Use only a modest amount of overdrive to get the benefit of sustain while preserving the guitar's natural tone.

Ex. 4

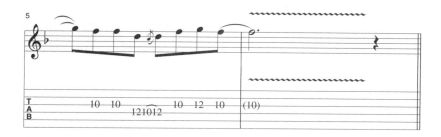

Much of the appeal of early blues music was in the banging, unpolished tone of players on acoustic guitars. Characteristically, Clapton brings elements of classic blues to his acoustic playing while refining the presentation. Stripped of the electric guitar's drive, sustain, and ease-of-play, Clapton gets the most out of an acoustic with a confident grip, chugging right-hand rhythms, and his typically discriminating note choices. Rhythmic playfulness makes this solo entrance work, where double-stops slide into position high on the neck (**Ex. 5**). Playing the slides without a pick attack changes the syncopation and gives the part an offbeat feel.

Ex. 5

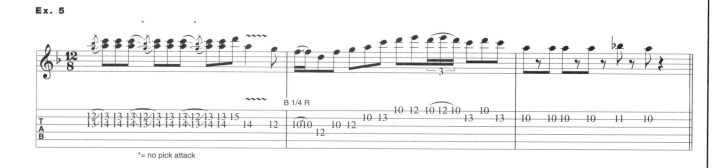

*= no pick attack

CHAPTER 3 Jimi Hendrix

Most people think of Jimi Hendrix as the primary purveyor of soaring psychedelic rock, a pyrotechnic master who took the electric guitar to places no one had ever imagined. Yet Hendrix's mind-bending progression from relative unknown to universal guitar hero was built solidly on the blues. He utilized the style throughout his career, eventually adding jazz, hard rock, and even fusion to the mix before returning to purer blues music near the end of his life. His playing inspired many of the guitarists in this book to extend their own horizons, including contemporaries like Clapton and Page, disciples like Stevie Ray Vaughan, and even elder statesmen like Buddy Guy.

BIOGRAPHY

Johnny Allen Hendrix was born on November 27, 1942, in Seattle, Washington. Several years later, after his parents split up, his father changed the boy's name to James Marshall Hendrix—shortened to "Jimi" as his career was first taking off.

His early musical influences were gleaned from his father's record collection, which consisted of albums by R&B and blues legends such as Muddy Waters, Guitar Slim, Chuck Berry, and B.B. King. Jimi picked up the guitar around age 12 and as a teenager played with various groups in and around Seattle. When he turned 17, Hendrix enlisted in the Army, joining an airborne division as a paratrooper. Injured while parachuting, he was discharged after two years.

Determined to take a stab at music, Hendrix established himself as a session man using the name Jimmy James. During the early '60s he backed artists such as King Curtis, the Isley Brothers, and Little Richard, in the process mastering the essence of blues, soul, and R&B. Directly influenced by Buddy Guy, Jimi also developed a performing style that drew attention not only to his playing but to his stage presence. And like Guy before him, Hendrix was told by his employers to keep his showmanship and more outrageous inclinations in check. Deciding to make it on his own, he moved to New York in 1964 and immersed himself in the burgeoning Greenwich Village blues and folk scene. Playing as Jimmy James and the Blue Flames, he performed covers of blues standards by Robert Johnson and Muddy Waters. He then teamed with seminal white blues singer John Hammond Jr., and the two played together until Hendrix was introduced to Chas Chandler, who had played bass in the Animals. Chandler offered to be Hendrix's manager and take him to England to create a band for him.

In 1966, with bassist Noel Redding and drummer Mitch Mitchell onboard, the Jimi Hendrix Experience made its debut. The trio's first full-length release, 1967's *Are You Experienced*, single-handedly changed the sound of rock 'n' roll and made Hendrix a worldwide sensation. The record showcased Hendrix's fascination with experimentation and sound effects as he pushed the limits of what the electric guitar was capable of. Additionally, Hendrix's songwriting and singing talents—untapped prior to the Experience—showed that he was more than just the planet's newest guitar hero.

Soon after the album's release, Hendrix and the band gave a legendary performance at the Monterey Pop Festival, where Jimi—looking to go over the top with his showmanship and acting on a guitar tech's recommendation—attacked his guitar and then burned it with lighter fluid. Surprisingly, it was during live performances such as this that Hendrix's blues side was on full display. Extended jams, blues covers, and originals like "Red House" showed how Hendrix could take something as straightforward as the blues and push it into new territories.

Aside from his live jams, Hendrix's recorded blues outings were fleeting and flirtatious; far more of his blues output has been released posthumously than he allowed in his lifetime. While the blues and its legacy of guitar heroes were fundamental to Hendrix's development as a guitarist, he was interested in pushing the boundaries of all kinds of music.

Within a year, the Experience had released both *Axis: Bold as Love* and *Electric Ladyland*. These albums found Hendrix venturing further into the sonic stratosphere, but his ties to the blues were still evident. On selections like "If 6 Was 9," "Gypsy Eyes," and "Voodoo Child (Slight Return)" he can be heard tie-dyeing the blues into an entirely new fabric. The songs featured a uniquely Hendrix approach, which can perhaps best be described as "acid-fueled blues."

Hendrix's reputation, and his love of experimentation, led him to jams with people ranging from Johnny Winter to John McLaughlin. Such ventures made him eager to incorporate other styles and musical viewpoints into his music. He put the Experience on hiatus in 1969, and then appeared at the first Woodstock festival. His interpretation of "The Star Spangled Banner" remains one of the most riveting and bombastic guitar solos ever performed.

Hendrix's restless nature led to the formation of Band of Gypsys with drummer Buddy Miles and bassist Billy Cox. The group recorded a live New Year's Eve show at the Fillmore East that was highlighted by "Machine Gun," a tune that demonstrated just how far Hendrix was pushing the notion of guitar playing. The landmark live album *Band of Gypsys* would be the fourth and final release of his lifetime.

Looking to create a permanent studio home for his experiments, Hendrix began working on Electric Ladyland Studios in New York City. Jimi was apparently ready to take the next step in his career—whatever that might have been—when he died after overdosing in his girlfriend's London apartment. The date was September 18, 1970. He was 27 years old.

GEAR & SETUP

It's hard to imagine Hendrix without his upside-down right-handed Fender Stratocaster. Instead of getting a left-handed guitar, he restrung the flipped-over Strat, keeping the knobs and trem bar up high on the body. At the time, the Strat was outfitted with one of the only whammy bars that could handle

CHECKLIST ✓

Guitar . . . . Fender Stratocaster

Neck . . . . Rosewood or maple

Condition . . . Standard

Setup . . . . Flipped over, restrung upside-down

Strings . . . . Fender Rock 'n' Roll medium-light (.010, .013, .015, .026, .032, .038), tuned down half- or whole-step

Pickups . . . . . . Stock

Picking . . . . . . Heavy pick; also used fingers

Amp . . . . Marshall 100-watt heads, Celestion-loaded cabs

Effects . . . . Roger Mayer Octavia, Univox Uni-Vibe, Vox wah-wah, Dallas-Arbiter Fuzz Face, studio effects

Tone . . . . Rich, thick; occasionally hollow; wet with effects

Signature traits . . . . Great tone; catching bass notes with thumb; heavy whammy-bar use; singing in unison with guitar

Tricks . . . . Tremolo dive-bombing; feedback; string-scraping; toggle-switching; picking with teeth; playing behind head; banging on pickups; banging on guitar body

Influences . . . John Lee Hooker, B.B. King, Magic Sam, Muddy Waters, Howlin' Wolf, Buddy Guy

Overall approach . . . . Experimental, unbounded, tasteful

SELECTED DISCOGRAPHY

With the Jimi Hendrix Experience:
Are You Experienced (Reprise, 1967)
Axis: Bold as Love (Reprise, 1967)
Smash Hits (Reprise, 1969)
Electric Ladyland (Reprise, 1968)
Historic Performances at the Monterey International Pop Festival (Reprise, 1970; side 1 only)
Live at Winterland (Ryko, 1987)
With Band of Gypsys:
Band of Gypsys (Capitol, 1970)
Band of Gypsys 2 (Capitol, 1986)
Live at the Fillmore East (MCA, 1999)
Jimi Hendrix releases:
The Cry of Love (Reprise, 1971)
Rainbow Bridge (Reprise, 1971)
Jimi Hendrix: Blues (MCA, 1994)

RECOMMENDED CUTS

"Red House" (*Are You Experienced*)
"Hey Joe" (*Are You Experienced*)
"Voodoo Child (Slight Return)" (*Electric Ladyland*)
"Gypsy Eyes" (*Electric Ladyland*)
"Little Wing" (*Axis: Bold as Love*)
"If 6 Was 9" (*Axis: Bold as Love*)
"Machine Gun" (*Band of Gypsys*)
"Catfish Blues" (*Jimi Hendrix: Blues*)
"Belly Button Window" (*First Rays of the New Rising Sun*, MCA, 1997)
"Angel" (*The Cry of Love*)
Many of these tracks also appear on various Hendrix anthologies and "best of" collections

Hendrix's abuse, and he still purposely bent the bar to make it more comfortable. He played both rosewood- and maple-neck Strats, usually strung with light-gauge strings.

Although that upside-down Strat will forever be Hendrix's trademark, he became a gear junkie as soon as he could afford to be. In addition to the Gibson Flying V and Les Pauls he would occasionally play live, Hendrix is known to have owned, among other instruments, a Gibson SG, Gibson 330, Gibson Firebird, Mosrite electric dobro, Guild 12-string, Rickenbacker JG 12-string, Zemaitis 12-string, Hagstrom 8-string basses, Rickenbacker bass, and Gibson and Martin acoustics.

After the Strat, Hendrix's other signature piece of gear was the 100-watt Marshall stack (with Celestion speakers), and he put the amp manufacturer on the map. He initially used the head with two 4x12 enclosures, a setup that would eventually triple in size. His experimental nature led him to occasionally swap the Marshalls out for Sunn and Sound City amps, and in the studio any available equipment was fair game. Early in his career he used a Silvertone amp with a 2x12 cabinet, and he owned at least one pair of Fender Dual Showmans.

Hendrix considered no effect too obscure or too new to be included in his rig. He relied heavily on pedal pioneer Roger Mayer and used effects in the studio and onstage. He used Mayer's Octavia, a Dallas-Arbiter Fuzz Face, a Vox CryBaby wah-wah pedal, a Leslie rotating-speaker amp, and a Univox Uni-Vibe. He routinely played with his pedals' order in the signal chain to alter his sound; for instance, he would put the wah-wah before distortion to get distorted wah. The high-pitch feedback squeals he produced with ease were often the result of jacking up the guitar's volume and stomping on the wah-wah or Fuzz Face.

Forever in search of new sounds, Jimi was intrigued by studio technology and the possibilities it opened. Many of the effects heard on his recordings—flanging, echo, reverb, reverse guitar—were directed by Hendrix but applied by his engineers and producers.

STYLE & TECHNIQUE

The key to Jimi Hendrix's style and technique was imagination. While he absorbed influences from blues, soul, R&B, pop, folk, and rock, his talent was greater than the sum of those parts. He held the techniques of blues masters in high regard, but in his giant hands they were launching points: He used trem-bar dips and swells to mutate open-string trills; tortured bends measure after measure; exploited, not resisted, feedback; and held dissonances as if to establish a new definition of harmony. While bluesmen of old mimicked the rhythms of locomotives and washboards, Hendrix created the sounds of birds, spaceships, machine guns, and angels.

His innovations did not come at the expense of good taste. He knew when to keep rhythmic parts sparse so a vocal melody had its turn in the spotlight. Solos were packed with outsized licks and tricks, but he did not overplay or incorporate unnecessarily busy parts. His acid rock was appropriately frenetic; his ballad playing melodic and gentle.

Hendrix used the guitar's mechanics to affect his sound. The tremolo bar—today's "whammy bar"—had long been used by rock 'n' roll guitarists (notably Duane Eddy), but Hendrix changed it from a mere twangy vibrato tool to something essential. He used it with feedback to achieve extreme pitch drops, as well as to create effects such as the sounds of a blitzkrieg. He took advantage of the Strat's multi-position pickup switch, rapidly toggling it between "on" and "off" settings to make the guitar stutter like a machine gun. Jimi was one of the first string-scrapers, scratching his pick down the low strings' outer winding to achieve metallic screeches.

Those were some of his more conventional tricks. Like Buddy Guy and other notable bluesmen before him, Hendrix used the guitar as a visual part of his performance. He played it behind his neck, behind his back, with his teeth, lying on his back. He beat it with his hand, thumped it against his hips, smashed it on the stage, and set it on fire. In a lesser player, these antics might have been dismissed as pure showmanship, but Hendrix made them part of his music. Though his entire repertoire has been studied and imitated by most every rock guitarist, it should be remembered that Hendrix did it all upside-down and backward, 35 years ago.

LESSON

A slow 12/8 blues provides plenty of open space in which to expand and experiment. **Ex. 1** is based on a simple vamp in open position. It starts with a bent 6th-string *G* immediately into a trill on the 4th string. Keep your right hand swinging (as shown in up/down strokes in the first bar) to get the right feel. This groove is down and dirty, so you can let the chokes fall where they will and let open strings ring even when you strike them haphazardly. The use of scooped strings (see the "x" notations in third full bar, denoting a slide from the 3rd fret to the 17th fret on the second string), chokes, and bends in place of "normal" notes are characteristic of Hendrix's blues-rock approach.

Ex. 1

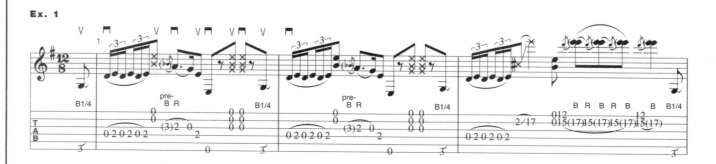

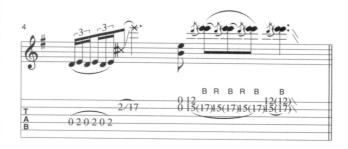

Hendrix turned noise—unpitched sound—into music. **Ex. 2** exhibits a favorite technique involving muted strings and the wah-wah pedal. Rather than trying to match your foot to what your hands are doing, simply rock the wah-wah up and down just as you would to keep time. Strum the first two bars with a lightly swinging syncopation on choked strings. Continue keeping time with your wah foot as the riff enters high up the neck. As in the choked opening, the accents throughout are on beats *one* and *three*. The two-bar figure repeats, with a small variation on the tail end.

Ex. 2

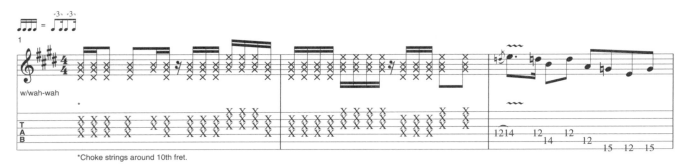

*Choke strings around 10th fret.

Jimi Hendrix was a fan of R&B guitarist Curtis Mayfield, crediting him with the sweet double-stops Hendrix borrowed for many ballads. Double-stops dressed up with suspensions, hammer-ons, and slides can be great tools for implying chordal harmony while avoiding stock barre fingerings. In **Ex. 3** the line between rhythm and lead playing is blurred in an *Em–G–Am–Em* progression. Begin in 7th position with a standard *Em* shape. After landing on the 5th-string *G*, establishing the change, jump to 3rd position for the double-stop that implies *Gsus4*. Barre straight across the top four strings of the 5th fret for the next bar of *Am*, catching the open bass note before the double-stop series, all of which falls in position. The last bar lands back on *Em*, with double-stop 4ths sliding up a step and back.

Ex. 3

As the centerpiece in a trio, Hendrix often had to fill both rhythm and lead roles. **Ex. 4**, from the rock end of the blues-rock spectrum, showcases a number of techniques on which Hendrix relied. It opens with *E* bends and a brief lick in *E* pentatonic minor. One-bar fills then follow a repeated figure on *E7♯9*—often referred to as the "Hendrix chord." Three of the four fills rely heavily on the whammy bar.

Ex. 4

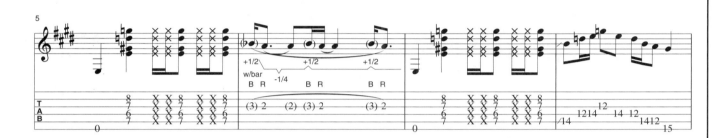

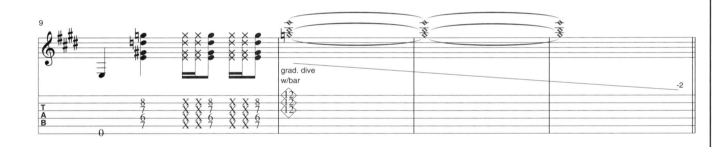

CHAPTER 4 Jimmy Page

▶ Jimmy Page is the guitarist who turned blues-rock into hard rock, creating concrete from the fluid riffing of blues players. Well versed in many blues styles, he used them to great effect on the earliest Led Zeppelin albums. Page's eclectic tastes and songwriting style ultimately led him on a musical path far removed from the blues, but he has returned to it time and again over the course of his long career.

BIOGRAPHY

James Patrick Page was born on January 9, 1944, in Heston, England. Like many other British boys of the 1950s, Page was listening to black bluesmen on the radio and on LPs he could find. At 15, after hearing Elvis Presley's "Baby Let's Play House," Page picked up the guitar and began playing with local skiffle and blues bands. He hooked up with neighbor Jeff Beck in several of these groups, but his generally poor health kept him from making a full-time commitment to any particular band. Instead, he decided to dedicate himself to art school.

But the allure of the guitar and the reputation he had acquired led him back to music—as a session player. He soon became one of a handful of studio guitarists who played on countless pop sides produced in England in the mid-1960s, from Tom Jones to the Kinks.

In 1964 the Yardbirds asked Page to fill the position left vacant by Eric Clapton, who had become disenchanted by the group's increasingly experimental pop style. Not willing to give up a lucrative session career, Page passed and recommended Beck for the role. Beck took the job and two years later asked Page to be the Yardbirds' bass player. Page agreed, but before long he had switched roles with guitarist Chris Dreja. As co-guitarists, Page and Beck developed a dueling lead style that mesmerized British club-goers and enthralled listeners. During this time, the Yardbirds produced commercial psychedelic pop that showed little evidence of the band's blues roots.

The Yardbirds were already falling apart by the time Page arrived. Beck left a year later, and Page managed to keep the band together until summer 1968. The group finally imploded with a string of unplayed dates booked. Page took advantage of the demand and formed the New Yardbirds, soon to be known as Led Zeppelin. Although similar in concept to the bands that both Clapton and Beck had formed post-Yardbirds (Cream and the Jeff Beck Group, respectively), Page played down his "guitar hero" role in Zeppelin, instead building the band on the rhythm section, primarily John Bonham's drums. The result was a sonic barrage that would elevate rock from its blues roots into the world of hard rock and heavy metal.

The first two Zeppelin albums were rife with blues-rock riffs and soloing. The band covered blues gems like Willie Dixon's "You Shook Me" and "I Can't Quit You Baby," adapted Dixon's "Bring It on Home," and borrowed entire phrases from artists like Howlin' Wolf and Albert King. Zeppelin's cover of "Bring It on Home" encapsulated the change from blues to rock more than anything else ever put on record, as Page mimicked Delta-style blues playing to near perfection before the song exploded into a distorted riff and drum blast that were unlike anything bluesmen could have imagined.

On other early Zeppelin cuts, Page used slide guitar—part of his very large bag of tricks—to evoke the blues. Tunes such as "What Is and What Should Never Be" and "You Shook Me" proved he understood the heart of the blues at the same time he was experimenting with new styles and technology. Once the capabilities of a state-of-the-art studio were at his disposal, Page's talents as a producer would affect the Zeppelin sound almost as much as his guitar playing.

By the third Zeppelin album, Page and company had moved beyond the blues to explore American folk and Celtic styles. Yet *Led Zeppelin III* showcased Page's finest blues piece, "Since I've Been Loving you." The slow-building blues tune features Page grinding out a solo that foreshadows the hard-rock solos that would eventually supplant the grooves and short phrases of blues solos.

For the most part, Page's blues leanings were left behind as he progressed into other musical forms, styles, and rhythms that were influenced by Celtic, Middle

CHECKLIST ✓

Guitar ....Fender Telecaster

Neck ....Stock

Condition .....Stock

Setup ....Stock

Strings..........Ernie Ball Super Slinky (.009, .011, .016, .024, .032, .042)

Pickups ....Stock

Pick...............Herco heavy

Amp ....Fender Twin Reverb, Supro

Settings ....Pushed to near meltdown; overdriven and loud

Effects..........Wah-wah pedal

Tone ....Bright, trebly

Picking ....Pick held between thumb and index finger

Attack...........Light but constantly moving; few rests or pauses

Signature traits ....Long, uninterrupted solo passages; lots of pull-offs; shimmering vibrato

Tricks............Mostly miking effects for blues

Influences ....Scotty Moore, Sonny Boy Williamson, B.B. King, Robert Johnson

Overall approach .....Frenetic and raw—don't sweat the details

Eastern, and African music. Nonetheless, he revisited the blues at later points in the Zeppelin catalog ("Tea for One" from *Presence*) and on his post-Zeppelin work ("Humming-bird" from *Outrider*, "Pride and Joy" from *Coverdale/Page*, and "Blue Train" from *Walking into Clarksdale*).

GEAR & SETUP

Jimmy Page was constantly experimenting with his setup, choosing amps and guitars from a substantial arsenal to achieve a variety of sounds. Rarely did he stick with one particular combination. While Page is associated with the Les Paul more than any other guitar (and perhaps vice versa), much of the classic Zep material was recorded with a Fender Telecaster. This was especially true on the earlier, bluesier albums, when he relied on the Tele running through a Supro amp. Interestingly, he's one of the few artists in this book—along with Roy Buchanan and Albert Collins—to stay away from the Strat. All three relied on Teles for the blues. Page also used Fender amps and Vox AC30s in the studio and in rehearsals during his Yardbirds and earliest Zeppelin days.

Live, all of this eventually gave way to the Les Paul and the fabled Marshall stacks, although he also used Orange cabinets. But for Page and the blues, it was pretty straight-forward: run a Tele through a Supro, crank it up hot enough to get some distortion, set the pickup switch to the bridge position, and take off.

Light-gauge strings, notably Ernie Ball Super Slinkys, contributed to the overall treble sound.

STYLE & TECHNIQUE

While he is considered one of the greatest lead guitarists, Page possesses a style that's considerably dirtier than most of his peers'. He's quite content to leave in pick clicks, string squeaks, slippery and skipped notes, and other assorted raw elements that would never make their way onto, say, a Clapton record.

Page is at his heart a rhythm guitarist, even if he's playing

SELECTED DISCOGRAPHY

With Led Zeppelin (all on Atlantic):
Led Zeppelin (1969)
Led Zeppelin II (1969)
Led Zeppelin III (1970)
Jimmy Page releases:
Outrider (Geffen, 1988)
Compilations and collaborations:
Session Man: Vol. 1 (Bomp!, 1991)
White Boy Blues, Vols. 1 & 2 (Castle, 1992)
The Firm (Atlantic, 1985)
Coverdale/Page (Geffen, 1993)
Walking into Clarksdale (with Robert Plant; Atlantic, 1998)

RECOMMENDED CUTS

"I Can't Quit You Baby" (*Led Zeppelin*)
"You Shook Me" (*Led Zeppelin*)
"Since I've Been Loving You" (*Led Zeppelin III*)
"Bring It on Home" (*Led Zeppelin II*)
"What Is and What Should Never Be" (*Led Zeppelin II*)
"Prison Blues" (*Outrider*)
"Writes of Winter" (*Outrider*)
"In My Time of Dying" (*Physical Graffiti*)
"Pride and Joy" (*Coverdale/Page*)
"Blue Train" (*Walking into Clarksdale*)

riff lines, so his emphasis is always on the phrasing and pacing. His right hand is typically doing a lot more work than his left. The most notable of his churning blues-rock riffs are played more as chords than single-note lines, employing double-stops and heavily attacked strings. Page is an exceptional fingerstyle player as well as flatpicker, which made him a more interesting acoustic player than some of his contemporaries.

Page's blues tone is tinnier than that of many other blues-rock players, indicating a heavy use of the bridge pickup and tone controls in the most trebly settings.

His effects came from a variety of sources, including creative microphone placement and the use of tape tricks. Overdriven amps, usually augmented by reverb or tape echo, did most of the work on his blues numbers. Page's pedals were not as liberally applied to his earlier blues cuts as they were on his later work, and they played little role in his blues-rock sound.

Page used a wide array of open and alternate tunings in his playing, influenced in large part by folk guitarist Bert Jansch. These include *DADGAD*, open *E* (*EBEG#BE*), and the less common *DGCGCD* (on "The Rain Song"). He was also one of the first proponents of the Transtuner bridge system, which allowed him to switch to new tunings with the press of a button.

LESSON

Though Jimmy Page did not rely heavily on the bottleneck, his occasional slide playing was expertly executed. Uncommon for his lead work, the round midrange tone Page used for slide is more in line with traditional blues recordings. The slow and carefully intonated slide part in **Ex. 1** is a blues line you might expect to hear played on a muted trumpet or trombone. To keep unwanted string tones from ringing while you're playing slide, let your 1st and 2nd fingers damp the strings; they should rest lightly on the strings behind the finger wearing the bottleneck.

Ex. 1

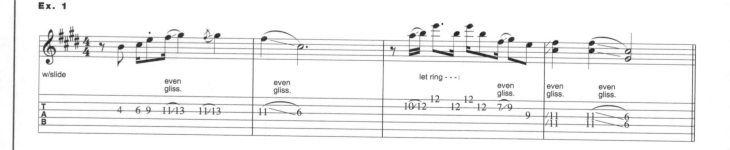

Power and bombast are signatures of Page's oversized riffing, and low-key blues compositions explode in his hands. **Ex. 2** stacks three guitar parts to convert a blues figure into a heavy, howling riff. First, Guitar 1 plays a 16th-note figure in open position, helped by hammer-ons from open strings to fretted notes. Guitar 2 enters to double Guitar 1—though in another position—and Guitar 3 closely matches the figure one octave higher. Characteristic of Page's arranging smarts, this kind of stack imbues a simplistic blues riff with heavy-metal power. When each guitar hits the bend (beat *three* of each bar), the parts can't help but separate a bit, spreading the riff wide.

Ex. 2

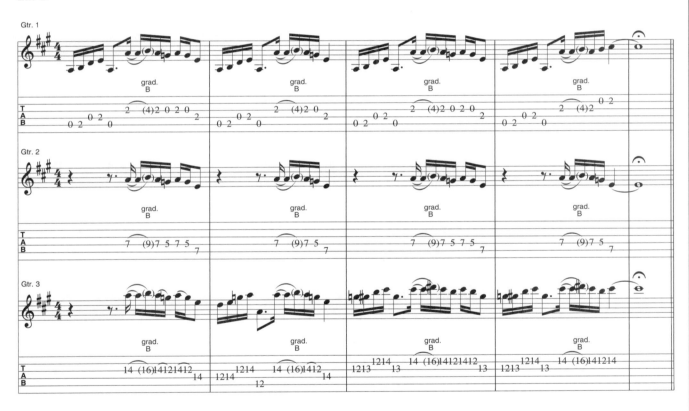

Page will be remembered for strutting onstage in front of a Marshall wall, but he knows how to lean back into a slow groove like a Southern bluesman in a rocking chair. His take on select Willie Dixon tunes finds him in purist mode, as heard in **Ex. 3**. Plunking out a prototypical blues figure in a moderate shuffle, Page does not leave open position for several bars, slowly building tension. The lilting *E5–E6* change with a light palm mute is a classic blues rhythm move, while the rolling *G–G♯* figure on the 6th string gives the lick forward movement.

Ex. 3

A slow tempo and sparse accompaniment open the space for a blues-rock guitarist to stretch out. Page's approach to tunes like "I Can't Quit You Baby" and "You Shook Me" is steeped in the tradition of electric blues, where a slow 12/8 begs the guitarist's indulgence. **Ex. 4** begins with a laid-back feel on the top strings. At the end of the first full bar, Page bends the 2nd-string *C* up one step then—without striking it again—bends it up another half-step before its whining release. After a lengthy rest and a change of pickup, a fast line bursts in. Page is famously loose with the timing of lead lines like this, and the beat is almost lost in the freneticism. It's only when he decelerates at the end of the line that he's back in tempo, landing on his feet.

Ex. 4

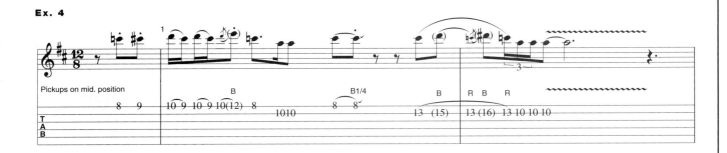

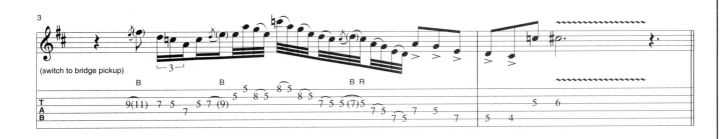

CHAPTER 5   Duane Allman

Duane Allman's legend is based on only five years of recording. In that time, he progressed from a sought-after blues-rock sideman to one of the world's most electrifying lead guitarists. His slide style set a standard that has never been surpassed, and his performance on *At Fillmore East* is considered by many to be the finest concert recording of any blues-rocker ever. His legendary status is all the more amazing given that he did all of his recording in his late teens and early 20s.

BIOGRAPHY

Howard Duane Allman was born on November 20, 1946, in Nashville, Tennessee. His father died when he was young, so Duane was exempted from serving in the Vietnam War. As a teenager he and younger brother Gregg headed to California to try their hands in the music business. Calling themselves the Allman Joys and then Hour Glass, they released two albums that went nowhere. This was due in part to the record company not liking the band's direction and refusing to release their third album.

Duane headed back to the South while Gregg remained in California. Showcased in various bands, Duane's superb guitar work landed him sessions at Fame Studios in Muscle Shoals, Alabama, where he played on a number of R&B records, starting with Wilson Pickett's *Hey Jude* in 1968. Pickett, taken by the young guitarist's sunny disposition, gave Duane the nickname Skydog. Joining the famed Muscle Shoals Rhythm Section, Duane cut tracks with Aretha Franklin, King Curtis, and Boz Scaggs, developing a stunning versatility in a number of musical styles and incorporating them into what would become his signature sound.

While studio work kept Duane busy, he craved being part of a band. His chance came when Capricorn Records founder Phil Walden asked Duane to record for him. Cobbling together bandmates from various groups and calling brother Gregg home from California, Duane built the Allman Brothers Band. Their performances became extended musical jams featuring raw blues, R&B, rock, and traces of jazz and psychedelia over the course of several hours.

Maintaining a grueling tour schedule, the band quickly became the preeminent purveyors of Southern-based blues-rock. This was due in no small part to the powerful dual-guitar interplay of Duane Allman and Dickey Betts. Their ability to trade leads and play harmony off of each other is evident on tunes like "Revival" and "In Memory of Elizabeth Reed." The duo's formula for multi-guitar blues-rock would be copied by almost every Southern rock band that followed.

Despite his commitment to the Allman Brothers Band, Duane was continually invited to play on albums by other artists. The most significant invitation came from Eric Clapton, who was recording with a group of old session friends in the band that came to be known as Derek & the Dominos. Allman joined the group for the now-legendary "Layla sessions," contributing as a full member. (He wrote the opening riff to the Clapton masterpiece "Layla.") However, Duane's first love was the Allman Brothers Band, and he turned down an offer to tour with Clapton and the Dominos.

In 1971 Duane and the band took time off from the road and sessions to begin recording their fourth album, *Eat a Peach*. On October 29, Duane swerved his Harley-Davidson to avoid hitting a truck in an intersection. He sustained severe head and torso injuries, and after three hours of surgery, the young guitar master died. He was 24 years old.

GEAR & SETUP

During his session days Duane played a Fender Telecaster and Stratocaster through a Fender Twin Reverb, along with other Fender amps. When he formed the Allman Brothers Band, he and Dickey Betts both used Gibsons almost exclusively, starting with ES-345s and SGs, which they would occa-

CHECKLIST ✓

Guitar .... Gibson Les Paul

Neck .... Standard

Condition ... Stock

Setup .... Standard

Strings ...... Heavy, .012–.058

Amp .... Fender Twin Reverb, Marshall

Settings ..... Overdriven, full volume

Picking ...... Light touch, circular style. Fingerpicked with thumb, index, and middle fingers for slide

Tone .... Bright treble

Attack .... Controlled

Signature traits .... Slide on ring finger, long solo passages, melodic slide

Tricks .... Sliding past highest frets; imitating harmonica

Influences ... Muddy Waters, Robert Johnson, Blind Willie Johnson, Elmore James, Taj Mahal

Overall approach .... Tasteful, clean, fluid

sionally trade between each other. Allman switched to Gibson Les Pauls and Marshalls when the band started touring, preferring the Les Paul's fatter tone—particularly on the neck pickup—coupled with the Marshall's distortion. Duane played a variety of Les Pauls, including gold-tops and Standards. He continued to use Fender amps in the studio.

Some of Duane's Gibsons were outfitted (and retrofitted) with fat-sounding PAF (Patent Applied For) humbucking pickups. While Betts used 100-watt Marshall heads, Allman used 50-watt Marshalls, which he could overdrive at lower volumes. He completed his Marshall setup with 4x12 cabinets outfitted with JBL speakers instead of the standard Celestions.

STYLE & TECHNIQUE

Like his brother Gregg, the left-handed Duane learned to play the guitar right-handed. This gave him a strong fretting and slide hand, which he used to great effect. His bends and vibratos are especially outstanding, as was the use of his fretting pinky (a finger all but ignored by players like Clapton). His left-hand dexterity also lent his slide playing additional speed and control.

Since he picked with his non-dominant right hand, Duane had a lighter touch than blues-rockers such as Roy Buchanan and Stevie Ray Vaughan— Duane's combination of masterful fretting with a softer picking hand contributed to his singular sound. This was further enhanced by his picking technique. Instead of flatpicking across a string, he tended to roll the pick at an angle, in an almost circular motion, across the strings. This softened the attack and helped keep his right-hand technique light.

Allman will be best remembered for perfecting the marriage of the slide with the electric guitar. While numerous players—including Albert Collins—had done it earlier, no one accomplished the range of tones, sounds, and emotions that Allman coaxed from his slide playing.

SELECTED DISCOGRAPHY

With the Allman Brothers Band
(all on Polydor):
The Allman Brothers Band (1969)
Idlewild South (1970)
At Fillmore East (1971)
Eat a Peach (1972)
With Wilson Pickett:
Hey Jude (Atlantic, 1969)
With Aretha Franklin:
Spirit in the Dark (Atlantic, 1970)
This Girl's in Love with You (Atlantic, 1970)
With Boz Scaggs:
Boz Scaggs (Atlantic, 1969)
With Otis Rush:
Mourning in the Morning (Cotillion, 1969)
With Derek & the Dominos:
Layla & Other Assorted Love Songs (Atco, 1970)
With Ronnie Hawkins:
The Hawk (Cotillion, 1971)
With various artists:
Anthology (Polygram)

RECOMMENDED CUTS

"Revival" (*Idlewild South*)
"Whipping Post" (*At Fillmore East*)
"Statesboro Blues" (*At Fillmore East*)
"Hot 'Lanta" (*At Fillmore East*)
"Stormy Monday" (*At Fillmore East*)
"One Way Out" (*Eat a Peach*)
"Trouble No More" (*Eat a Peach*)
"Mean Old World" (*Anthology*)
"Shake for Me" (*Anthology*)
"Loan Me a Dime" (*Boz Scaggs*)
Many of these tracks also appear on various Allman Brothers Band anthologies and "best of" collections

Inspired by Taj Mahal to pick up the slide, he started by wearing a glass Coricidin bottle on his ring finger. The small cold-remedy container didn't span the entire width of his Les Paul fretboard, so Duane's nimble left hand stayed busy jumping the bottle from string to string. It also limited him to playing triads when he used the slide for chords. When playing slide, he picked with his thumb, index, and middle fingers.

To prevent sympathetic string noise and buzzing, Allman used his middle finger to dampen the strings behind the slide. He also set his action fairly high, as many slide players do, to prevent the strings from being pressed against the frets. Given the strength of his fretting hand, the higher action may not have posed as much of a problem as it would have for most players. There is some anecdotal evidence that he also wrapped his strings over the bridge (not on the grooved pins) to get better sustain out of each note.

To get the most out of his slide playing—for both chording and solos—Duane frequently used open tunings, notably open E (*EBEG#BE*). You can hear this tuning on "Statesboro Blues," "One Way Out," the live version of "Trouble No More," "Stand Back," and "Little Martha."

Duane's warm tone indicates less reliance on the bridge pickup, coupled with rolling the treble off the neck pickup. Like Clapton, though, he was a knob twirler, constantly fiddling to get the right tone and volume. On his live work, you can hear him pulling the volume down at the end of solos as he prepares to switch back to rhythm playing.

A remarkable electric soloist and slide player, Allman was also a nimble acoustic player, a fact best showcased on "Little Martha."

QUICK TIPS ON PLAYING SLIDE LIKE DUANE

- Wear the slide on your left (fretting-hand) ring finger.
- Keep the slide perpendicular to the neck—that is, parallel to the frets. Angling it will put you off pitch.
- Play the notes by placing the slide over the fretwire. In normal fingering, you play between frets, but playing directly over the fretwire is the only way to get notes in tune with a slide. Good intonation is the mark of a professional slide player.
- Don't press down.
- Let your left middle and/or index finger rest lightly on the strings behind and parallel to the slide. This prevents unwanted string tones and buzzing.
- In palm-muting fashion, rest the outside edge of your picking hand against the strings.
- Pick using your thumb, index, and middle fingers. When those fingers are not picking a note they should be muting the string.
- Don't sit still on a note. Either slide off or add vibrato.

LESSON

Players using a slide on an open-tuned guitar tend to hover around the key's home positions. **Ex. 1** is in the key of *D*, so 10th position is a good base. The lick begins with the chromatic climb up to 10th position, with the picking alternating between adjacent notes on the 2nd and 3rd strings. Concentrate on nailing the 2nd-string notes, as they get the accents; the 3rd-string notes are barely articulated. In bar 2, notes descend in pairs until the return to 10th position, where an octave *D* jump resolves the phrase.

Ex. 1

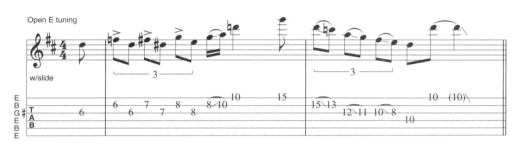

Duane Allman had dozens of signature slide tricks. One of his bluesiest and most unusual was to make his guitar sound like a harmonica, with the aid of his honking lower-midrange tone. **Ex. 2**'s rapid move involves skating the slide back and forth on the 3rd and 4th strings. Let both strings ring on the descending slides but mute them on your way back into position.

Ex. 2

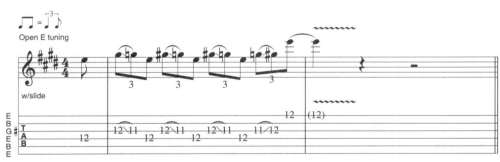

Southern blues was imprinted on almost every note Duane played, and pure blues occasionally poked through his rock exterior. The slide part in **Ex. 3**, again in open *E*, is best played on acoustic guitar (better yet, a Dobro) and uses the I–V–IV–I changes at the end of a traditional 12-bar blues. The riff for each change is essentially identical, just moved to a different home position. Slide into place on the lower strings, letting the low chord tones ring as long as possible before the riff forces you out of position. Considering how much music this example creates, it requires relatively little effort or movement.

Ex. 3

Duane Allman and Dickey Betts were masters at arranging for double lead guitars. When the two paired up on a riff, Duane's slinky slide was the perfect foil to Dickey's burpy staccato playing. Dickey kept his guitar in standard tuning while Duane often added his parts in open *G* (*DGDGBD*), open *D* (*DADF♯AD*), or open *E* (*EBEG♯BE*).

To understand how Duane and Dickey wove parts together, first consider a Betts-like part. **Ex. 4** is a simple *G* pentatonic riff played in 3rd position.

Ex. 4

Now retune your guitar for Duane's part as shown below in **Ex. 5**. (Open tunings are convenient for slide players because the slide, barring straight across the strings, rests on chord tones.) Start with the slide barring at the 8th fret. Pluck the 2nd string with your middle finger, being careful to sound only the *G* note. It's tougher still to get back to this position after you've struck the 3rd-string *D*; you can get some 2nd-string sliding on your way, but be sure to mute that 3rd string with your index finger. Incidental notes like the *B* in the sixth bar add some great slide color.

On the accompanying CD track, Betts's part from Ex. 4 is heard in the left speaker and Allman's part (Ex. 5) on the right.

Ex. 5

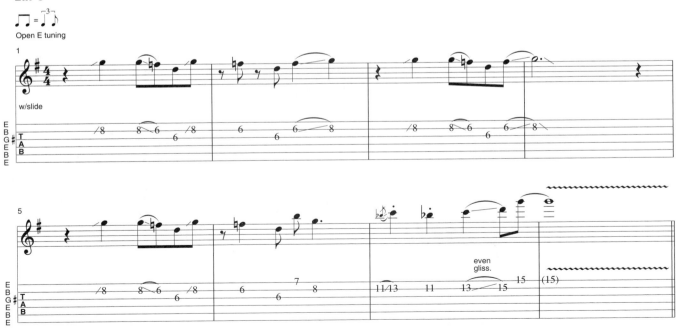

CHAPTER 6   Albert Collins

Albert Collins was one of the few blues-rockers to become identified with a singular signature sound that followed him throughout his career. His steely Telecaster tone and rapid, stinging lines weren't fiery like those of his peers; they had the cold edge of a jagged icicle. His brand of blues-rock earned him the nickname the Iceman, a title he wore with pride.

BIOGRAPHY

Albert Collins was born on October 1, 1932, in Leona, Texas. His parents were farmers who moved around the state, ultimately settling in Houston. Inspired by his cousin, the legendary Lightnin' Hopkins, and fellow bluesmen John Lee Hooker and Gatemouth Brown, young Albert dabbled in blues, primarily on piano and organ. Ultimately he picked up the guitar in his teens, learning on a cigar-box contraption before getting one of the early Epiphone hollowbodies. When he acquired a solidbody Fender Esquire, though, he found a guitar more to his liking. Collins became intent on creating an electric blues sound that would be his alone.

Performing in Southern juke joints, Collins was one of the first players, along with Buddy Guy, to push the blues so hard they rocked. Both of these guitarists, growing up in the shadow of Hooker and the three Kings (Albert, Freddie, B.B.), set themselves apart with a more aggressive approach to electric guitar and a wildness in their techniques and performances.

Collins recorded tunes for small independent labels and had his first regional hit, "The Freeze," in 1958. The sound of that instrumental tune came to define him for the rest of his career—a snarling, percussive, almost shrill tone that pierced through the entire band. His guitar wailed as if it were being tortured.

Collins played up his icy side by making enough temperature references in his song and album names to wear out a weatherman: "Frosty," "The Freeze," "Defrost," "Sno-Cone," "Ice Pickin'," "Cold Snap." He reinforced his persona in his live shows, where his 150-foot cord allowed him to walk out into the audience.

Like many black bluesmen, Collins was overlooked by major record labels and the general public during his early career. That changed in 1968, when he was "discovered" by the members of blues-rock jam band Canned Heat, who produced three albums for him on Imperial. Adding his own vocals, Collins set out to win new fans. By this time he had switched to a genuine Fender Telecaster, the guitar with which he would be associated for the rest of his life.

Moving to California, Collins began a nonstop tour of the Pacific Coast. By 1974, though, he decided it wasn't working for him. He wasn't cracking into the big time, even though his shows had become huge draws. Everyone who heard his playing raved about it—but he personally was fed up. Collins gave up the guitar and found work as a construction worker, signing on with a crew that was hired to fix Neil Diamond's house. The irony was not lost on Collins or his wife—who was his chief songwriter—and they decided that music was what Collins had to do, regardless of the level of success he might achieve.

Albert returned to active duty in 1978 when he was signed to Alligator Records. Suddenly, the world realized what it had been missing. Like the best of the blues-rockers, he found that his career had been given a second act. Now known as the Master of the Telecaster, the Razor Blade and, most famously, the Iceman, Collins was finally recognized for the unique stylist he'd always been. He didn't play slow, sultry, crying-in-your-beer blues. He played sharp electric blues-rock that slapped you in the face, left your ears ringing and your skull vibrating. This was blues you had to rock to.

Over the rest of his career, Albert worked with or dueted with some of the best names in the business, including Johnny Copeland, Gary Moore, Eric Clapton, Stevie Ray Vaughan, David Bowie, and even avant-garde sax man John Zorn. Collins won W.C. Handy and Grammy awards, and was invited to play at LiveAid. Never one to rest on his laurels, Collins took advantage of his newfound fame and worked hard to keep it. He played right up until he was diagnosed with in-

CHECKLIST ✓

Guitar . . . . Fender Telecaster

Neck . . . . Maple

Condition . . . Beat-up

Setup . . . . Standard

Strings . . . . Mixed set (010, .013, .015, .026, .032, .038), tuned to *Fm*

Pickups . . . . . . Stock bridge pickup; Gibson humbucker in neck position

Amp . . . . Tube amps, primarily a 4x10 100-watt Fender Quad Reverb

Settings . . . . . Overdriven and loud, treble and mids boosted, bass low

Effects . . . . Reverb

Tone . . . . Shrill, high, icy

Picking . . . . . . Used thumb and first two fingers exclusively

Attack . . . . Percussive; pulled and popped strings; quick stabs

Signature traits . . . . Phrases grouped in short clusters; popping strings; pull-offs snapped against neck; stinging clear notes; wide vibrato

Tricks . . . . Neck capoed on high frets

Influences . . . Lightnin' Hopkins, John Lee Hooker, Gatemouth Brown

Overall approach . . . . Searing, loud, always electric, favoring a rock approach over a blues approach

operable lung cancer. Collins died on November 24, 1993. He was 61 years old.

GEAR & SETUP

Although Collins's first solidbody electric guitar was a 1952 Fender Esquire, he found his kindred spirit in the evolution of that guitar, the Telecaster. While his earlier Teles had a single pickup in the bridge position, his favorite axe came to be a blond maple-neck 1966 Tele outfitted with a Gibson humbucker in the neck slot. He most often played with the pickup switch in middle position, splitting the bridge pickup's brightness with the humbucker's fullness. You can also hear him switching to the bridge pickup's trebly bite in the middle of a solo.

For his amplification—and much of Collins's sound was about amplification—he went through a 100-watt Fender Quad Reverb. The Quad was similar to the Twin Reverb except that it featured four 12" speakers instead of two. Collins set his Quad to overdrive with the treble set all the way up and the bass almost nonexistent. He kept the reverb on to add a little chill to his riffs.

Collins used a capo up high on the neck, mostly on the 5th, 7th, 9th, and even the 12th fret. The capo served the additional function of keeping his light-gauge strings nice and taut.

STYLE & TECHNIQUE

A combination of several uncommon techniques and devices produced the Iceman's sound. His phrases were alternately percussive and fluid, he muscled unusual timbres with his right hand, and his tone was like a taste of cold metal.

The two most important factors in Collins's approach are his open *Fm* tuning and his use of the capo. Collins played his entire repertoire with the alternate tuning *FCFA♭CF* (low to high), which incorporates the three notes of the *Fm* triad. He changed keys by moving the capo to

SELECTED DISCOGRAPHY

The Complete Albert Collins (Imperial, 1970)
Ice Pickin' (Alligator, 1978)
Frostbite (Alligator, 1980)
Frozen Alive! (Alligator, 1981)
Showdown (with Johnny Copeland and Robert Cray; Alligator, 1985)
Iceman (Virgin, 1991)
Collins Mix: The Best of Albert Collins (Pointblank, 1993)
Live 92/93 (Pointblank, 1995)
Deluxe Edition (Alligator, 1997)
Rockin' with the Iceman (Culture Press, 1998)

RECOMMENDED CUTS

"Frosty" (*Live 92/93*)
"If Trouble Was Money" (*Deluxe Edition*)
"The Moon Is Full" (*Collins Mix: The Best of Albert Collins*)
"Don't Lose Your Cool" (*Collins Mix: The Best of Albert Collins*)
"Honey Hush" (*Collins Mix: The Best of Albert Collins*)
"Things I Used to Do" (*Frozen Alive!*)
"Got a Mind to Travel" (*Frozen Alive!*)
"Collins' Mix" (*The Complete Albert Collins*)
"Backstroke" (*Rockin' with the Iceman*)
"Cold Cuts" (*Deluxe Edition*)

F MINOR TUNING

The Iceman always tuned his guitar to open *F* minor—*F* minor is the chord heard when he strummed his open strings. Here is how to retune from standard, shown from the lowest string to the highest.

Standard	Retune	*F* Minor
E	up ½ step	F
A	up 1 ½ steps	C
D	up 1 ½ steps	F
G	up ½ step	A♭
B	up ½ step	C
E	up ½ step	F

Retuning considerations

Collins used a mixed set of string gauges to accommodate the upward tuning. You may want to consider doing the same, or using a light-gauge set to avoid breakage and relieve some of the tension on your guitar's neck.*

When reading music in alternate tunings, use the tablature, relying on the standard notation only for rhythms and note durations. Otherwise the search for every note would be exasperating on the retuned strings. If you opt not to retune your guitar and attempt these examples in standard tuning, read the standard notation exclusively.

Collins used a capo, placing it on the neck according to the song's key. For these examples, the tablature is shown in relation to the capo. When you see an "O" on a tab line it does not indicate a true open string but a note stopped by the capo. A "1" indicates one fret above the capo, "2" is two frets above the capo, and so on.

Blues scale in *F* minor tuning

Follow the tab in **Ex. 1** to see what a blues scale looked like to Albert Collins. (Be sure to retune your guitar to open *F* minor first, and capo as shown.) Notice how many unfretted notes are included. With his combination of capo and alternate tuning, he played the blues as if in open position.

Ex. 1

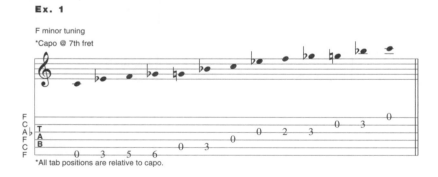

F minor tuning
*Capo @ 7th fret

*All tab positions are relative to capo.

* Shortcut: If you're concerned about changing your strings' gauges or retuning so far up, tune to *E♭* minor (*E♭B♭E♭G♭B♭E♭*). This way, no string is retuned more than a half-step. Then capo one whole-step (two frets) higher than instructed in the examples. You can play the tab and match the pitches on our CD this way because the tab is shown in relation to the capo.

the appropriate fret, a technique he learned from Gatemouth Brown. This allowed him to transpose immediately and still use the same signature licks.

Also crucial to his sound—though difficult to recreate—was his right-hand technique. Collins picked with his thumb, forefinger, and middle finger much like a banjo player. He didn't use his ring and little fingers except to damp the strings. This "claw" technique helped Collins pop the strings—grabbing them from below, pulling up, and then releasing. This gave him a percussive snap in a style more identified with funk bassists. Collins, however, sought to emulate the brassy attack of a trumpet; his notes' sting was accentuated by a liberal dose of reverb.

Collins played loud and aggressively, like Roy Buchanan, but he usually limited his solo phrases to short, intense blasts, rarely playing lines longer than a few bars or even a few notes. When he did cut loose, he would solo with a flurry of well-articulated notes interspersed with long sustained tones. He seldom strayed more than five frets from the capo, played the vast majority of lines on the top four strings, and rarely used double-stops. His left-hand technique was fairly standard blues, with little to no use of the little finger. The pull-offs that often followed his right-hand snaps increased the sharpness of his attack. He executed a huge vibrato with a side-to-side shake of his wrist.

Much of Collins's rhythmic sensibility came from his early piano- and organ-playing days. His rhythm playing was sparse, perhaps due to his challenging *Fm* tuning, and it resembled the stabs of a Hammond B-3 organ more than the steady ratta-tat of right-hand guitar flailers. His chord voicings also held more in common with organ players than guitarists.

LESSON

Albert Collins's technique of snapping the strings against the fretboard gave his playing a percussive edge. Plus, with the capo high up the neck, he got more mileage out of the technique using pull-offs between open and fretted strings. To put the string-spank into **Ex. 2**, get your index finger under the 3rd string

Ex. 2

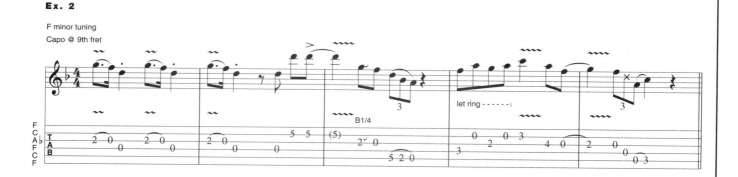

on the first note of the opening phrase, and pull up hard. (If you prefer to attempt the example with a pick, get the tip under the bottom side of the string and use an upstroke.) Catch the third note (*D*) on the adjacent string with your thumb. Collins put his signature on his licks by presenting them in lightning-fast blasts and putting space between them.

Ex. 3's phrase opens with bends and pull-offs played primarily on the 2nd string. Then two similar phrases played in open position are heard in a brief question-and-answer sequence. A lot of notes are packed into each cluster, and they seldom ring over one another. Because Collins did not use a pick, he was able to damp strings with available right-hand fingers. Let any fingers that are not picking notes rest on the strings.

Ex. 3

Though he was well equipped to deliver speedy passages, Collins relied on far more than a quantity of notes for impact. Articulate delivery, contrast among phrases, and the use of unfilled time contributed greatly to his blues power. His fingers-only approach helps provide the gentle opening of **Ex. 4**. The quiet is then cut with a sharp line, further contrasted by the pickup change from middle

Ex. 4

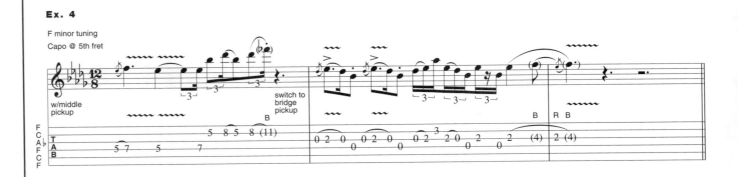

to bridge position. Get your forefinger under the 3rd string for the snap on E♭, and attack the open 4th string hard with your thumb as well. For the whole-step bend at the end, brace behind your 2nd finger with your 1st.

While it may seem like a headache to find blues chord changes in open *F* minor tuning, the trick is not recreating standard-tuned voicings. Rather, the tuning brings notes within reach that otherwise would never make it into a conventional chord shape. **Ex. 5**, representing a full blues progression, incorporates unconventional voicings, but you'll see that the fingerings are actually simpler and involve fewer fretted notes than standard-tuned changes. Notice also how the tuning provides octaves in parallel fingering.

Ex. 5

F minor tuning
Capo @ 7th fret

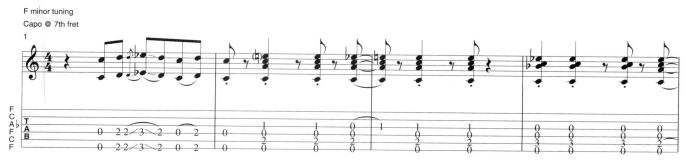

CHAPTER 7 Roy Buchanan

Roy Buchanan, revered by fellow musicians but underappreciated by the masses, was probably the most reluctant blues-rocker ever to pick up the guitar. He lived one of the strangest lives of any respected guitarist since Robert Johnson, yet he is still barely known by the general public. Like Eric Clapton, all he ever wanted to do was to get to the heart of the blues. But whenever his guitar prowess threatened to metamorphose into fame and fortune, Buchanan ran away from the limelight until he could re-emerge in some little-scrutinized side project. His life as a preeminent blues-rocker mirrored that of his pure blues forebears, and his incredible talents and his peculiar lifestyle make him one of the most intriguing guitarists to ever play the blues.

BIOGRAPHY

Leroy Buchanan was born on September 23, 1939, in Ozark, Arkansas. His father, a farmer and sometime Pentecostal minister, moved the family to Pixley, California, soon after Roy was born. There, at the age of seven, Roy was taught how to play lap steel guitar, country-style. When he turned 13, he bought a Fender Telecaster—because to him it sounded like a steel guitar. As his playing progressed, he switched to a Les Paul and then a Stratocaster, but he ultimately made his way back to the Telecaster. For Roy, this was like the prodigal son having found God in his own way. But for the rest of his life, it was demons that would chase Roy, and they'd almost always get the upper hand.

He left home when he was 15, playing in bands all over the United States, predominantly in the bars of Bible Belt states like Oklahoma and Arkansas. Along the way, he absorbed massive amounts of gospel, blues, country & western, rockabilly, R&B, and everything else he came into contact with. He listened to Scotty Moore, Buck Owens, Johnny "Guitar" Watson, and Barney Kessel. During a stint in L.A., jump-bluesman Johnny Otis took an interest in Buchanan that led Roy to study with Watson and James Brown mainstay Jimmy Nolen. In time, Roy became known to the cognoscenti as the most eclectic blues-rocker in the country.

After starting his own band, the Heartbeats, Buchanan got notable sideman gigs with Dale Hawkins (of "Suzie Q" fame) and later with Dale's cousin, Ronnie "the Hawk" Hawkins. Ronnie was a near-legendary wildman known for singing searing R&B in clubs from the American South on up to Canada. Possessing a knack for attracting undiscovered talent, Hawkins hired Buchanan in the late 1950s. Buchanan's intense playing dovetailed perfectly with Hawkins's sound, and Roy helped nurture the talents of the younger members of the band, notably Robbie Robertson. But in a pattern to be repeated throughout his life, Buchanan called it quits with Hawkins just as the band was making it big. Buchanan said it was because he didn't like having to put showmanship over musicianship for Hawkins's fans, while Hawkins and others said that Roy was just too strange—he had allegedly said that his skill came from being part wolf. Upon Roy's departure, Robertson was promoted to lead guitar. Eventually Robertson and the other Hawks joined Bob Dylan and found fame as The Band.

Buchanan, on the other hand, found himself playing the bar circuit, ultimately settling with his family in the Washington, D.C., suburbs in 1961. There, his reputation as a purist began to grow. He formed and disbanded numerous groups, the first of which he called the Snake Stretchers. While his contemporaries gained fame, Roy and his band slogged it out doing one-night stands with a constantly changing cast of characters.

Roy's life was a bizarre blend of the crazed and the composed. In addition to signing up as a sideman with one unknown after another, Buchanan enrolled in barber college to try to make ends meet. A seemingly introverted man, he drank heavily and did copious amounts of drugs, yet he stood nearly stock still while playing onstage, refusing to let the appreciative crowds move him. For his live performances he dressed like a refugee from a lumber camp, always wearing an odd assortment of coats and hats, offset by his Vandyke beard.

His appearance made it even more difficult for people to believe that this man could make his beat-up Telecaster scream the way it did. His instrumentals were composed of lengthy solos that sounded like vocals or horns as they amazed local audiences night after night. Eventually the D.C. press caught up with him, followed by *Rolling Stone* and finally PBS, which filmed a documentary based on Roy's performances called *Introducing Roy Buchanan*, which through urban legend has come to be known as *Introducing the World's Greatest Unknown Guitarist*.

The exposure brought opportunity, unbidden, to Buchanan's doorstep. Polydor signed him, but his five albums for the company did little to improve his personal fortune. Atlantic took him on in 1975, but the pattern was repeated: Roy created three blues-rock albums that sold poorly but were coveted by his circle of fans. Notable among his releases was *Loading Zone*, featuring Booker T. guitarist Steve Cropper, bassists Stanley Clarke and Will Lee, and a host of other impressive musicians. But Roy's style was so eclectic that listeners didn't know how to tag him—nor did the record companies.

Ever appreciated by fellow musicians, Buchanan's playing influenced Jeff Beck, who dedicated the monumental "'Cause We've Ended as Lovers" to Roy on *Blow by Blow*. The Rolling Stones allegedly offered Buchanan the lead-guitar spot after Brian Jones died, though that may be another of the myths that surround Roy's life. Along the way, Roy mentored other players, including rising guitar master Danny Gatton, a player whose relatively anonymous life paralleled Buchanan's.

Every step of the way, though, Buchanan insisted on being accepted for making music his own way. Unfortunately, his recording career was increasingly spotty, and after a decade of not getting recognition on his own, he quit the music business. Blues label Alligator coaxed him out of retirement in 1985, allowing him to deliver what he felt were his best recordings. He went on to win the 1986 Grammy for Best Blues Album.

But Buchanan's personal demons, the likes of which were normally associated with old-time blues players, finally caught up with him. On August 14, 1988, he was arrested for public drunkenness in Virginia. That night, depending on whom you believe, he either hung himself or was a victim of manhandling by the police. He was found dead in his cell the next morning. He was 48 years old.

Buchanan's style was hard-charging, like the man himself. There is nothing delicate about his playing. Among blues-rockers, the only other player to go at the guitar as aggressively or with the same amount of speed was Stevie Ray Vaughan. Even on mid-tempo tunes, Buchanan took his overdriven Tele and burned up the tracks. When he played slowly, he gave the music an urgency that made it feel like it was moving faster than it was. Nothing in his playing, or his life, seemed to have been done at anything less than full throttle.

GEAR & SETUP

Roy Buchanan relied on Telecasters his entire career, notably a 1953 and a 1983. In his later years he mixed and matched necks and bodies across a variety of Teles, many from the '50s, and outfitted some of them with Bill Lawrence pickups.

CHECKLIST ✓

Guitar . . . . Fender Telecaster

Neck . . . . Maple

Condition . . . Beat-up, mix and match

Setup . . . . Standard

Strings . . . . Light, .009–.040

Pickups . . . . . . Bill Lawrence

Pick . . . . Heavy

Amp . . . . Fender Twin Reverbs, Fender
Vibrolux, Peavey Classic

Settings . . . . . Overdriven; low reverb

Effects . . . . Boss DD-2 Digital Delay
(later in career)

Tone . . . . Razor-like, trebly

Picking . . . . . . Standard thumb/index technique;
hybrid technique; circular picking

Attack . . . . Aggressive

**Signature
traits** . . . . Pinch harmonics, volume swells,
wide vibratos, deep bends. Sparse,
stabbing rhythms

Tricks . . . . Swells, pickup tapping, behind-nut
bends

Influences . . . Scotty Moore, Buck Owens,
Jimmy Nolen, Johnny "Guitar"
Watson, Barney Kessel

**Overall
approach** . . . . Hard, abusive, full-out

SELECTED DISCOGRAPHY

Buch and the Snake Stretchers
  (Bioya, 1971)
Roy Buchanan (Polydor, 1972)
That's What I Am Here For
  (Polydor, 1974)
In the Beginning (Polydor, 1974)
Live Stock (Polydor, 1975)
Loading Zone (Atlantic, 1977)
When a Guitar Plays the Blues
  (Alligator, 1985)
Dancing on the Edge
  (Alligator, 1986)
Hot Wires (Alligator, 1987)
Guitar on Fire: The Atlantic Sessions
  (Rhino, 1993)
Deluxe Edition (Alligator, 2001)

RECOMMENDED CUTS

"The Heat of the Battle" (*Guitar on Fire: The Atlantic Sessions*)
"Green Onions" (*Guitar on Fire: The Atlantic Sessions*)
"The Messiah Will Come Again" (*Guitar on Fire: The Atlantic Sessions*)
"Fly ... Night Bird" (*Guitar on Fire: The Atlantic Sessions*)
"Ramon's Blues" (*Guitar on Fire: The Atlantic Sessions*)
"Judy" (*Guitar on Fire: The Atlantic Sessions*)
"Jack the Ripper" (*The Alligator Records 25th Anniversary Collection*)
"When a Guitar Plays the Blues" (*Deluxe Edition*)
"Flash Chordin'" (*Deluxe Edition*)
"Chicago Smokeshop" (*Deluxe Edition*)

He played most often through Fender amps, primarily Twin Reverbs and a Vibrolux, although he used a Peavey Classic as well. Overdrive and a touch of reverb helped make his razor-sharp tone rich and sustained.

His signal was unadulterated by effects, as he preferred getting uncommon sounds with a variety of right-hand techniques. However, after his comeback in the mid-'80s, he used a Boss DD-2 Digital Delay to fatten up his sound. He also gave up the Tele long enough to incorporate a Gibson Les Paul into his arsenal during the 1980s (a Les Paul actually graces the cover of *Hot Wires*). But the Les Paul was very much a later and secondary addition to his collection, and though he also was known to perform with a Stratocaster, his mainstay was the Tele.

Roy used light-gauge strings on his Tele but practiced with heavy-gauge strings on his Martin acoustics. Like Albert Collins, his lead tone was stinging and bright.

STYLE & TECHNIQUE

Buchanan is regarded for his lead playing, but it was his good ear and appreciation of rhythm that made his lines soar. He practiced by finding scales up and down the neck to match chord tones, and he punctuated his leads with the rhythms he heard bassists and drummers play. He knew how to "arc" a solo, filling it with gradually increasing tension until it burst open at its peak. He then would return to the starting point before entering another chorus.

Like Clapton, he reached for emotion in the blues, and there is real passion and thoughtfulness in his playing: not classic blues sadness or lamenting, but raw agony, pain, and even ecstasy. His familiarity with other types of roots music, from country & western to gospel, helped him expand beyond straight blues. Buchanan let his guitar express all the things that he as a person probably could not.

Roy made his Tele squawk, scream, hiccup, yowl, and beg for mercy. His repertoire is full of surprising sounds, most of them resulting from inventive and resourceful right-hand techniques. Rather than relying on outboard effects, Buchanan discovered the wide potential in his Telecaster's built-in electronics. He is famous for his violin-like volume swells (a technique players like Eddie Van Halen were using almost three decades later), in which he strikes a note with the guitar's volume knob all the way down and then eases the volume up with a free finger. He was fond enough of the technique that he would usually play with some volume in reserve—i.e., at 6 or 7 rather than 10—so headroom would be available for the swells. Occasionally he would employ that technique using the tone pot rather than the volume, bringing single notes or, more commonly, chords to full bloom with a swell of treble.

Roy also made liberal use of pinch harmonics, which his Tele's electronics enhanced. Whereas true pinch harmonics involve "pinching" the string between the finger and pick, Buchanan achieved his effect by getting some of the flesh of his right-hand thumb into his picking attack. Depending on where the right hand is placed over the string, striking it with half-pick/half-thumb allows the fretted note's overtones to produce a squealing, multi-timbred sound.

Buchanan found a great sound by combining these two techniques (volume swell and pinch harmonic) with a bend. He would strike a pinch harmonic with the volume down, then bend the string upward with his left hand as he rode the volume pot with his right. The resulting bluesy, vocalesque cry graces numerous Buchanan leads and has been emulated by rock and blues guitarists for years. This technique made his guitar sound like everything from a crying baby to a shrieking woman to a chirping bird.

He did not reserve bends for this technique alone. His bends may often sound wild and flailing, but Buchanan was well in control when bending far beyond a whole-step or applying multiple bends to one pick stroke. He clamped his 2nd and 1st fingers behind the 3rd for wide bends, and he would also put muscle behind the bend from his forearm rather than his wrist. Always getting the most of the bluesy tones between half-steps, Buchanan would often strike a pre-bent note before easing it down into fretted position, or even attack a note in bent position without ever easing the tension.

Buchanan built up his left-hand strength by practicing on acoustics and then performing on the Tele, a guitar known to be unforgiving. Bent notes and heavy vibrato were part of Roy's technique bag, as were the hammers and pull-offs he used to imply speed. He didn't consider himself a fast player, although his mastery of technique qualifies him as one of the earliest shredders, and certainly one of the only blues-rock shredders.

Buchanan's early studies on steel guitar informed his playing throughout his career. In addition to volume swells, Roy found he could emulate the steel guitar's multi-string bends by reaching behind the nut and depressing the short lengths of string between the nut and the tuners. Unlike most electric guitarists, he also mimicked steel guitar by using his right-hand fingers in conjunction with the pick. This hybrid technique paid off for both rhythm and lead playing: For leads he would hold the pick between his thumb and index finger and incorporate plucked notes with his middle and ring fingers; for rhythm he would use the pick and all three available fingers to control full chords.

His right-hand technique didn't stop there. He was also a master of circular picking, a technique that allows for very rapid, soft attacks. Rather than a wrist pivot, circular picking involves a rotation of the fingers. The pick, held at an angle rather than parallel to the strings, catches the string on its edge as it circles the string, striking repeatedly on angled downstrokes and upstrokes.

A few other signature Buchanan techniques involved tapping the pickups with his fingers, detuning a string till it was flopping and then picking aggressively, and snapping his fingers on the Tele's steel bridgeplate. While such techniques might be regarded as mere trickery in the hands of a lesser guitarist, in Buchanan's fingers they were all finesse.

LESSON

To play like Roy Buchanan you have to master the volume swell. The Telecaster's chrome speed-knob volume control is especially convenient for the technique because it can be adjusted easily with a single finger: just roll the knob along the side of an extended digit. Most guitarists will prefer to use the pinky on the volume pot because it has the farthest reach from the thumb and forefinger holding the pick.

The other volume swell trick is in the timing. Pick the note with the volume down, then immediately begin dragging up the volume with your pinky. The goal is to remove the picking attack but still hear the note at its peak volume.

Once you get comfortable with volume swells, try combining them with other techniques and applying them to familiar licks. The Buchanan-style passage in **Ex. 1** includes several applications, including single notes, chords, pre-bent notes, and a brief eighth-note melody line.

Ex. 1

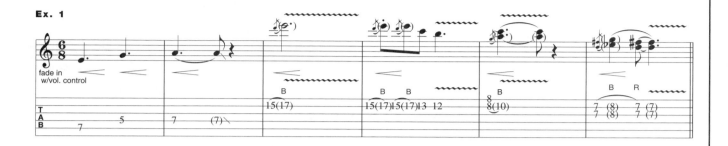

Milking the soul from a slow blues, Buchanan could soar over the changes with crying, legato lead lines. Played in 15th position, **Ex. 2**'s *G* minor passage opens with a bent and quivering high *C*. In Buchanan style, torture the note, hanging *just* below *C* on the initial upward bend and the *C* is in bar 2. Patiently—dragging the time a bit—release the bend and descend until you're riding the half bend on *D* with your 1st finger—tougher than the high bend because there are no extra fingers for backup.

Ex. 2

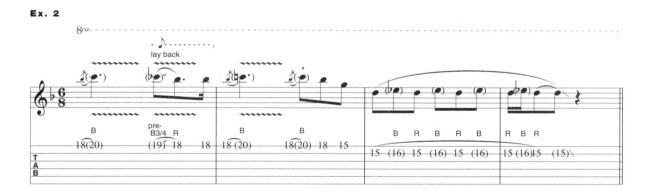

Buchanan urged countless knocks, squeaks, and oddball timbres from his Tele, though never at the expense of good taste. Begin with **Ex. 3**'s fast-picked run up the 3rd string, letting the fleshy outer edge of your right-hand palm rest against the strings (notated as "P.M." for palm mute) while your left hand slides up and down the neck on indefinite pitches. At the top, catch the high bend and then strike the triple-stop at the 13th fret for a quick falloff (which will sound familiar to Stevie Ray Vaughan fans). The last notes should be played with very hard downstrokes—pinched where you can—and land on the bent and shaking 5th-string *C#*.

Ex. 3

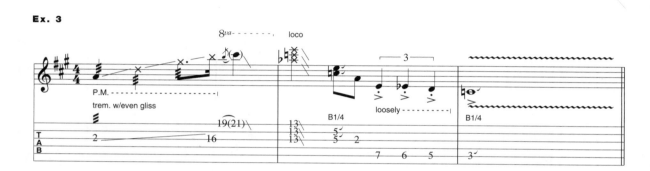

Buchanan was modest about the speed of his picking hand, and he often implied faster picking with left-hand hammers and pull-offs. The flurry of notes opening **Ex. 4** comes in very rapid groupings of six, but each group has only two pick attacks: one each on the 1st and 2nd strings. In bar 2, grip the 3rd-string *C* and bend up repeatedly before hanging on *D*. The last bar features a "touch harmonic," executed by gently tapping the string one octave higher than the note fingered. Your touch at the 17th fret should be over the fretwire, not the space between frets.

Ex. 4

*P.H. = pinch harmonics

CHAPTER 8 Stevie Ray Vaughan

No one drove rock further back into the blues than Stevie Ray Vaughan. Other blues-rockers did it the other way around; they started with the blues and applied electric rock to define their styles. Stevie approached the blues as an aggressive rocker, beginning with the experimentation of Hendrix and the passionate intensity of Clapton and then working his way back into the likes of Albert King and Howlin' Wolf. The approach set him apart from every other guitarist who has ever played blues-rock, but future blues-rock guitarists are more than likely to have a trace of SRV's influence.

BIOGRAPHY

Stevie Ray Vaughan was born on October 3, 1954, in Dallas, Texas. Along with his older brother, Jimmie, Stevie developed an early love of Texas blues. Both boys quit high school and left home as teenagers to pursue musical careers, gigging on the bar circuit that had in earlier days been the home of players like Albert Collins and Johnny Winter. Stevie formed a variety of bands such as Blackbird, the Nightcrawlers, the Cobras, and the Triple Threat Revue before hitting paydirt in 1978, when he created the trio Double Trouble. With drummer Chris "Whipper" Layton and bassist Tommy Shannon (a sideman of Johnny Winter's), the band ratcheted up the traditional sound of Tex-Mex blues. Their live show caught the attention of Mick Jagger, who invited the band to play a private party for the Rolling Stones. From there they were offered a spot at the Montreux Jazz Festival, where Vaughan's playing impressed Jackson Browne—who offered the band time at his recording studio—and David Bowie. Bowie, always on the lookout for virtuosic unknowns, asked Stevie Ray to join him as guitarist on his dance-infused pop album *Let's Dance*.

All of this was an unlikely career path for a Texas blues-rocker, but Stevie used his newfound mainstream fame to help put Double Trouble on the map. The band's first release, *Texas Flood*, arrived in 1983 along with *Let's Dance*, and the double shot put Vaughan front and center in the guitar universe. After falling out with Bowie at the US Festival, Vaughan devoted his time exclusively to Double Trouble, releasing *Couldn't Stand the Weather* and setting the standard for blues-rock from that point forth.

Vaughan was getting serious radio play, and his albums were spawning singles like "Look at Little Sister," from 1985's *Soul to Soul*. His shows, a mixture of intense blues with the kind of rock theatrics that Hendrix had perfected (playing behind his head, picking with his teeth) were non-stop sweatfests that drew big crowds. But the rigors of the road and the musician's lifestyle took their toll. Drink and drugs ate into Vaughan's ability to perform. He took time out to get himself clean, re-emerging in 1989 with *In Step* (which contained the radio staple "Crossfire") and recording an album with brother Jimmie, *Family Style*, for a fall 1990 release.

The night of August 27, 1990, Stevie Ray played a sold-out show in East Troy, Wisconsin, with Buddy Guy, Eric Clapton, Robert Cray, and Jimmie Vaughan. By all accounts, it was a stunning performance. Stevie left that evening in a helicopter, which crashed into a mountainside, killing all aboard. SRV was 35 years old.

GEAR & SETUP

Though he dabbled with other guitars, Stevie Ray Vaughan was overwhelmingly a Stratocaster player. His Strats were mixed and matched, largely because his aggressive playing style wore out components from pickguards to necks and regularly needed replacing. The guitars were named as he got familiar with the particular wear, tear, and sound of each one: Number One, Lenny, Charlie, Scotch.

He liked his Strats with rosewood fretboards and with the heaviest fretwire available; only bass-guitar frets could manage the workout Stevie gave his guitars with his strong hands and very heavy-gauge strings (.013–.060). Given the heavy strings and the high action Stevie Ray preferred, it's remarkable that he played with such speed and incorporated so many wailing, multi-string bends. He also tuned down a half-step, which helped him get a heavier and thicker sound than one would expect from a typical Strat setup. To gain wider tonal variations, he substituted 5-position pickup switches for the usual Strat 3-position. He used Fender's stock pickups, relying heavily on the neck pickup, with the middle and bridge pickups thrown in for variety. Taking a cue from Jimi Hendrix, he used a left-handed whammy so that the bar was anchored off the bass end (top side) of the bridge, and he tightened the whammy-bar springs to their limit.

Preferring the near-meltdown sound of heated tube amps, Stevie Ray ran his Strat through a variety of Marshalls, Fenders, and Dumbles—often recording with several at once. The Fenders were mostly Vibroverbs (a couple of the earliest ever produced, Nos. 5 and 6) and Super Reverbs. The Marshalls were varied: a few famed "Plexi" heads, a 100-watt Super PA and a 200-watt Major, as well as a JCM 800, running through modified Marshall cabinets. He also used Howard Dumble Steel String Singer 150-watt heads when he couldn't get replacement tubes for the Marshalls.

To push a lot of air and get a lot of power, Stevie used large speakers, typically 12's or 15's—the Vibroverb had a single 15" speaker, and the Super Reverbs were 4x10. He also used large Marshall 4x15 cabinets, sometimes driving them with Dumble heads.

His most employed effect was a wah-wah pedal, usually a Vox CryBaby. (Stevie owned at least one Vox wah that previously belonged to Hendrix). For buzzsaw distortion on solos, he employed a Fuzz Face. He also used an Ibanez Tube Screamer—not for distortion, but to boost his signal's gain. His one other notable effect came from a Fender Vibratone speaker cabinet, which employed a rotating foam baffle to create a Leslie-like swirling sound. You can hear this on "Couldn't Stand the Weather" and "Cold Shot."

STYLE & TECHNIQUE

Vaughan's sound can best be described as aggressive and passionate, yet he was supremely controlled. Even in the midst of a seemingly frenzied solo, Stevie Ray knew exactly where he was going and what he was doing. A master of the blues pentatonic scale, Vaughan could see beyond standard positions and dress up the blues with passing tones. He put his hands on the guitar in every way he

CHECKLIST ✓

Guitar . . . . Fender Stratocaster

Neck . . . . Rosewood fingerboard, jumbo frets

Condition . . . Mix and match

Setup . . . . High action; left-hand whammy bar, heavily sprung

Strings . . . . . . Heavy Bill Lawrence and GHS Custom, .013–.060; usually tuned down a half-step

Pickups . . . . . Stock; 5-position switch

Amp . . . . Fender Super Reverbs, various Marshalls, Dumbles

Settings . . . . Tubes overdriven with gain

Effects . . . . . Ibanez Tube Screamer (for gain), Dallas-Arbiter Fuzz Face (lead distortion), Vox CryBaby wah, Fender Vibratone cabinet

Tone . . . . Earthy, full, lots of low end with high-end bite

Pick . . . . Rounded edge

Picking . . . . . Fast and nimble; often tremolo style; circular picking

Attack . . . . . . Aggressive, almost abusive, but never sloppy

Signature traits . . . . Distinct tone; loco bends and lead-line rhythms; glissandos; hard shuffle grooves

Tricks . . . . . . Playing behind head, through legs; playing slide with right-hand ring over pickups

Influences . . . Howlin' Wolf, Albert King, Muddy Waters, B.B. King, Lonnie Mack, Jimmie Vaughan, Eric Clapton, Jeff Beck, Jimi Hendrix

Overall approach . . . . Blues harmonies and progressions played with a rock 'n' roll aggressiveness

SELECTED DISCOGRAPHY

With Stevie Ray Vaughan & Double Trouble (all on Epic):
Texas Flood (1983)
Couldn't Stand the Weather (1984)
Soul to Soul (1985)
Live Alive (1986)
In Step (1989)
The Sky Is Crying (1991)
In the Beginning (1992)
With the Vaughan Brothers:
Family Style (Epic, 1990)

RECOMMENDED CUTS

"Pride and Joy" (*Texas Flood*)
"Scuttle Buttin'" (*Couldn't Stand the Weather*)
"Couldn't Stand the Weather" (*Couldn't Stand the Weather*)
"Voodoo Chile (Slight Return)" (*Couldn't Stand the Weather*)
"Cold Shot" (*Couldn't Stand the Weather*)
"Look at Little Sister" (*Soul to Soul*)
"Crossfire" (*In Step*)
"Wall of Denial" (*In Step*)
"Little Wing" (*The Sky Is Crying*)
"Willie the Wimp (and his Cadillac Coffin)" (*From Dusk till Dawn* soundtrack, Sony, 1996)
Many of these tracks also appear on various Vaughan anthologies and "best of" collections

could, utilizing rakes, hammers, pull-offs, multi-string bends, ghost bends, palm muting, headstock chimes, whammy bends, and anything else that could make the instrument sing.

One of the keys to his technique was his articulation, the ability to make each note stand out on its own regardless of playing speed. This came from both a strong fretting hand and a fast but hard picking style. Stevie Ray had a dead-on sense of pitch bending; one of his trademarks is his ability to get several individual pitches from the same bent note, riding the bend up and back. The same finger strength that allowed him to perform these bends also gave him the ability to bend several strings at once and to push individual strings most of the way up the neck. He had the strength to bend those heavy strings not only with his ring finger, which can be supported by other fingers, but also with his index finger. Like Albert King, he would slap strings against the fretboard to create a stinging sound from individual notes. Vaughan's vocal style is also very similar to Albert King's.

Stevie Ray used both a pick and his fingers, although he used the rounded end of the pick instead of the point. This also took some of the treble out of his sound. He regularly employed a form of tremolo picking known as circular picking, or "figure eights." This added speed to his solos. From Lonnie Mack he learned to incorporate open-string pull-offs, and many of his fleet-fingered breaks and fills are played in open position. He often employed trills, mordents (single-note trills), and other ornamentation usually associated with classical music.

Stevie's approach to soloing was, by his own admission, motivated more by feel than anything else. Claiming not to have ever played anything exactly the same way twice, he made each and every solo count by having a thorough understanding of where the song was at every point in time, and then applying the appropriate notes. This can be heard in his live recordings, where he builds his solos over long jam sections. In the studio, his solos were almost always cut live without overdubs or edits.

LESSON

Stevie Ray could shuffle like nobody's business, emulating an entire band's rhythmic pulse in a single guitar part. The feel is all in the right hand. Three pointers will help get you on track with **Ex. 1**'s shuffle: Keep your strokes swinging on even eighth-notes (as shown at bar 1); rotate the hand in a circle as you strike the strings, bringing it closer to the neck on downstrokes, closer to the bridge on upstrokes; and strike *hard*.

The part sounds deceivingly simple. Be sure to keep the bass line walking steadily and catch details such as the choked upper strings combined with bass note (second upbeat), achieved by sliding into the *G#* without a pick attack.

Ex. 1

Playing predominantly in a trio setting, Vaughan was adept at merging chordal and lead parts. He was able to fill gaping holes in the rhythm while maintaining a fierce pace with his solos. Notice how **Ex. 2** states the *Bm* harmony in the opening with the introductory bass note, chord-tone double-stops, and an arpeggio outlining *Bm*. In the second two bars, an *Am* chord gets a similar treatment: the root is heard first, followed by double-stops.

Ex. 2

Ex. 3 is another instance of Vaughan's doing double duty on rhythm and lead, this time with more separation between the two. The driving rhythm part moves an *E9* chord in and out of position, building significant tension with the pair of triple-stops on top of *F9* at the end of bar 2. Breaking into a lead, the part then puts the open strings to good use for the Texas-style turnaround. The five-note figure at the end of bar 3 is simple to play considering the speedy fingers it implies. Simply slide down from the 4th-fret *B*.

Ex. 3

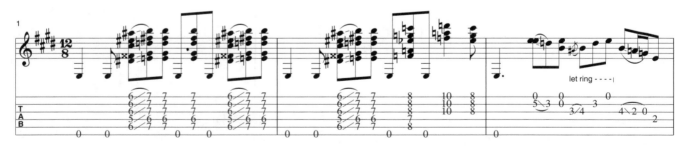

Ex. 4, a lead line over *Dm7*, gets its rolling feel from a series of triplets. Stay in 10th position for the length of the lick, backing up the *C–D* bend with adjacent fingers. Take your time with the bend so that it's just reaching the *D* at the end of the half-beat count. The example draws to a rapid, Buddy Guy–like close with the final 16th-notes. Light flanging (emulating Stevie Ray's Vibratone rotating-speaker effect) will give your tone a glistening sound.

Ex. 4

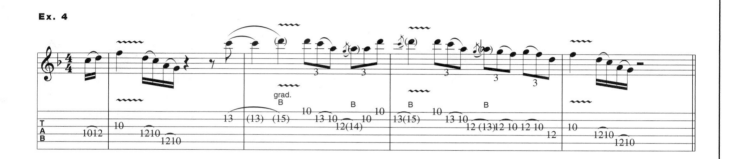

CHAPTER 9 Kenny Wayne Shepherd

Kenny Wayne Shepherd is a young man with a lot of time ahead of him. Yet his skill and his popularity show how newcomers can pick up the mantle left by their forebears and carry it forward. Nowhere in this book is that more true than in the case of Shepherd, who has been the only new blues-rock guitarist to earn the sort of acclaim bestowed on his predecessor, Stevie Ray Vaughan. In much the same way that Vaughan channeled Hendrix and Albert King, Shepherd is the incarnation of Vaughan. His playing is eerily close to that of SRV's, and KWS appears to have time to take blues-rock guitar to new places in the 21st century.

BIOGRAPHY

Kenny Wayne Shepherd was born on June 12, 1977, in Shreveport, Louisiana. His father was a radio DJ with a love of the blues and an extensive blues record collection, with discs by the likes of Hubert Sumlin, B.B. King, and Albert King. The boy had a revelation at the age of seven, when his father promoted a local concert featuring Stevie Ray Vaughan. Sitting on the side of the stage, KWS decided what he wanted to do with his life.

Kenny Wayne started teaching himself how to play the guitar, and he taught himself well. His first big gig was in New Orleans at age 13, a stellar performance that convinced him to start playing live on a regular basis. But his youth made him appear to be a novelty act, so he and his father, who became his manager, decided to get serious. Kenny made a series of recordings in Shreveport (including doing overdubs on an old Willie Dixon recording). He put together a band and toured fairs in and around Louisiana, eliciting raves for his intense and aggressive blues-rock style.

There had been an obvious void in the blues-rock world since the death of Stevie Ray Vaughan in 1990. Kenny's sound, his choice of tunes, and his setup were so similar to Vaughan's that comparisons became inevitable, but the kid still held his own. Industry buzz surrounded him, and he was signed by Giant Records in 1993.

His first record, *Ledbetter Heights*, was released in 1995, when Kenny was barely 18 years old. The record hit No. 1 on the *Billboard* blues charts, as did its 1997 follow-up, *Trouble Is . . . .* KWS became the new face of blues-rock, picking up where SRV had left off. The Kenny Wayne Shepherd Band opened for Van Halen, the Eagles, and the Rolling Stones, and Kenny was invited to be part of the first G3 tour, headlining along with guitar heroes Steve Vai and Joe Satriani.

The upstart from Louisiana went on to win several music industry awards, including *Billboard*'s Best Blues Album (*Trouble Is . . .*), and he earned a Grammy nomination. He released a live album in 1999, *Live On*, and then hooked up with Stevie Ray Vaughan's backing band, Double Trouble (drummer Chris Layton and bassist Tommy Shannon, plus SRV keyboardist Reese Wynans) for the Trouble Is Double Tour in 2001.

Still in his mid-twenties, KWS has reached musical heights rarely scaled by musicians twice his age. His association with Double Trouble and his three acclaimed albums have cemented his status as the blues-rock guitarist to watch. Unlike many of the people who have influenced KWS, he still has time on his side.

GEAR & SETUP

Kenny Wayne Shepherd's setup is almost identical to Stevie Ray Vaughan's. This was a conscious decision he made early on, and it has served him well.

Kenny Wayne sets up his Strats in imitation of SRV's guitars; among his favorites are a 1961 and a 1954 with a rosewood fingerboard. He outfits his guitars with graphite saddles (to reduce string breakage), a 5-way pickup switch, and a left-handed tremolo system à la Stevie Ray. The flip-flopped whammy helps keep him from accidentally jamming the bar down over the strings while playing. His guitars are refitted with big Dunlop frets (6100s), accommodating his heavy-gauge Ernie Ball strings (.012–.058), which he routinely tunes down a half-step.

Kenny uses a 100-watt 1965 reissue Fender Twin with two 12" Electro-Voice speakers, and a 100-watt Fender Vibrasonic with one 15. In addition, he occasionally plays through Fender Tone Master heads. All amps are cranked to 10 to get that near-meltdown sound, with the treble between 5 and 6 ½, mids between 5 and 8, bass down around 3 or 4, and reverb around 2.

Shepherd also takes his effects from the SRV playbook: an original 808 Ibanez

CHECKLIST ✓

Guitar . . . . Fender Stratocaster

Neck . . . . Rosewood fingerboard, jumbo frets

Condition . . . Mix and match

Setup . . . . Whammy bar on the bass side (up) of bridge

Strings . . . . Ernie Ball heavy (. 012, .014, .018, .028, .038, .058), tuned down a half-step

Pickups . . . . . . 3-position switches replaced by 5-position

Amp . . . . Fender Twin Reverbs, Vibrasonic, Tone Masters

Settings . . . . . Volume on 10; bass low

Effects . . . . . . Ibanez Tube Screamer, Dallas-Arbiter Fuzz Face (lead distortion), Vox wah-wah

Tone . . . . Raspy, deep

Attack . . . . Aggressive but controlled

Signature traits . . . . Arrhythmic bends, staccato breaks

Tricks . . . . Playing behind head, through legs

Influences . . . Stevie Ray Vaughan, Albert King, Muddy Waters, Jimmy Reed

Overall approach . . . . Aggressive, loud, favoring rock

Tube Screamer, Vox wah-wah, Dunlop Uni-Vibe, and a Roger Mayer Octavia.

STYLE & TECHNIQUE

Kenny Wayne has incorporated the techniques of many of his influences. He is perhaps a bit more studied than improvisational, drawing from existing examples rather than exclusively creating on the fly. His touch is a bit lighter than his heroes', and his lines are peppered with staccato phrases. Still, Shepherd gets the kind of low-end growl into his leads that's as dependent on a player's hands as it is on his gear. He has a strong left hand capable of wide bends and vibrato, and a fast picking hand for cleanly executed lines. His rhythmic placement and application of bends are distinctive, lending his solos an especially edgy sound and neck-jerk syncopation.

One of the reasons to listen to KSW is to see how blues-rock continues to evolve. With Clapton returning to roots blues, Kenny Wayne remains one of the only recording artists with a direct lineage to the kind of blues-rock that makes everyone in this book worth listening to in the first place.

LESSON

Kenny Wayne Shepherd's solos often show not only impressive chops but good melodic sense. **Ex. 1** comprises one entire chorus of an eight-bar shuffle. The repeated opening phrase over the I chord provides a hook with just three notes. Staying within 5th position in bar 3, Shepherd plays a chromatic descent (borrowed from the I chord's E blues scale) over the IV change, pivoting against a quarter-bent G♮ on the 2nd string in bar 4. He accentuates the change to the V7 chord (bar 5) with the solo's highest note, a 7th-fret B bent up one step. From here it's one last twist in 5th position before the quick change to open position for a classic blues turnaround. The turnaround phrase, alternating fretted notes with open strings before the chromatic climb from A to B, cues the band to the solo's conclusion.

Ex. 1

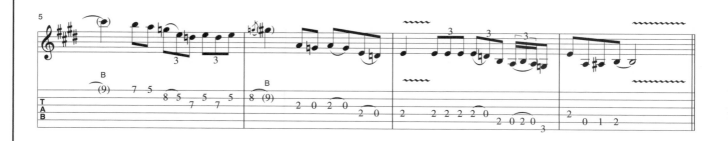

This passage from an *E* blues, like many Shepherd leads, intermingles quick lines with slow bends. **Ex. 2** opens on beat *three*, squeezing the 15th-fret *G* up a whole-step, back to position, then back up a quarter-step. The part hinges on good execution of this bend and the two that follow; the bluesiness comes from the way they stop the action to push slowly upward. Use the entire duration of the note shown to get from fretted to bent position. You want to tease the note toward its goal each time, just barely reaching pitch before releasing.

Ex. 2

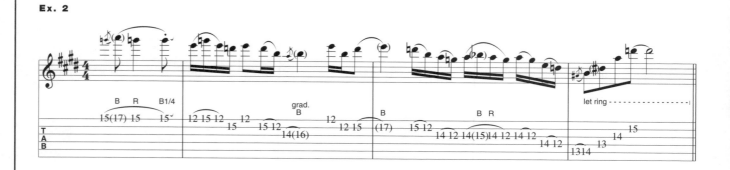

The tasteful application of double-stop hammers is the signature of many ballads by Stevie Ray Vaughan—and Hendrix before him, and Curtis Mayfield before him. In a great example of how young players can update blues-rock hallmarks, **Ex. 3** combines three double-stop moves in a harder, funkier context. The first comes on the first two strings in 3rd position; barre across the two strings and hammer the 2nd string two frets up. Bar 2 includes 7th-position double-stops, implying a chord change to *D*. It then comes down to 5th position for the double-stop hammer (marked by the grace note) over *C*. The short lick at the end gets you back into position to repeat.

If you keep your right-hand swinging steadily in eighth-notes, you'll naturally catch the chokes notated with X's below. This is a simple progression, but the hammers and the suspensions they imply provide plenty of tension and release.

Ex. 3

ON THE CD

Track 1: Tuning

Track 2: Buddy Guy Ex. 1

Track 3: Buddy Guy Ex. 2

Track 4: Buddy Guy Ex. 3

Track 5: Buddy Guy Ex. 4

Track 6: Eric Clapton Ex. 1

Track 7: Eric Clapton Ex. 2

Track 8: Eric Clapton Ex. 3

Track 9: Eric Clapton Ex. 4

Track 10: Eric Clapton Ex. 5

Track 11: Jimi Hendrix Ex. 1

Track 12: Jimi Hendrix Ex. 2

Track 13: Jimi Hendrix Ex. 3

Track 14: Jimi Hendrix Ex. 4

Track 15: Jimmy Page Ex. 1

Track 16: Jimmy Page Ex. 2

Track 17: Jimmy Page Ex. 3

Track 18: Jimmy Page Ex. 4

Track 19: Duane Allman Ex. 1

Track 20: Duane Allman Ex. 2

Track 21: Duane Allman Ex. 3

Track 22: Duane Allman Ex. 4

Track 23: Duane Allman Ex. 5

Track 24: Albert Collins Ex. 2

Track 25: Albert Collins Ex. 3

Track 26: Albert Collins Ex. 4

Track 27: Albert Collins Ex. 5

Track 28: Roy Buchanan Ex. 1

Track 29: Roy Buchanan Ex. 2

Track 30: Roy Buchanan Ex. 3

Track 31: Roy Buchanan Ex. 4

Track 32: Stevie Ray Vaughan Ex. 1

Track 33: Stevie Ray Vaughan Ex. 2

Track 34: Stevie Ray Vaughan Ex. 3

Track 35: Stevie Ray Vaughan Ex. 4

Track 36: Kenny Wayne Shepherd Ex. 1

Track 37: Kenny Wayne Shepherd Ex. 2

Track 38: Kenny Wayne Shepherd Ex. 3

Stratocasters, Telecasters, and Cyber-Deluxe amplifier provided by Fender Musical Instruments Corp.

All tracks performed by Rich Maloof and recorded at OopStudios, Brooklyn, New York, except tracks 6–7 and 28–31, performed by Pete Prown at Colonbleau Studios, Rose Valley, Pennsylvania.

Additional equipment provided by the authors and respective studios.

PHOTO CREDITS

Pages 14, 22, 40, 56, 74, 82: Ken Settle

Pages 30, 48: Joe Sia

Page 64: Chuck Pulin / Star File

ACKNOWLEDGMENTS

The authors wish to acknowledge the following for their help in creating this book:

Thanks to our editors at Backbeat Books, Richard Johnston and Nancy Tabor, for giving us the opportunity to put this book into place and for making it all worthwhile. That extends also to Philip Chapnick, who encouraged us to find a home for this book within his publishing group.

We would like to thank Bill Cummiskey of Fender Musical Instruments for the generous use of various Stratocasters, Telecasters, and other Fender equipment. Bill's extraordinary assistance in selecting appropriate instruments helped us emulate players' tones on the audio examples. We've matched guitars and amps with the original artists as closely as possible, and we could not have done it without him.

And finally, thanks must go to Pete Prown, fellow writer, friend, musician, guitar gear authority, and all-around good guy, for lending his playing to select—and difficult—tracks. Look for his books *Legends of Rock Guitar* (Hal Leonard, 1997) and the upcoming *Gear Secrets of the Guitar Legends* (Backbeat).

HP Newquist would like to thank:

First and foremost, I am grateful to Rich Maloof for his work in making this book a reality. It was a partnership in the best sense of the word, from the writing and editing to the creation of the music examples. Rich's audio and performing skills, however, are what made the accompanying CD a reality, and for that he deserves singular credit. His friendship—and his many talents—have always been invaluable.

Thanks to Trini, Madeline, and Katherine. They've always understood how important sitting down to write or sitting down to play is to me. But the importance of my books and my guitars pales in comparison to what these three women mean to me.

Finally, thanks to those individuals who taught me how to play guitar—and write a complete sentence—along the way. That goes from everyone in my family and my many bandmates on to all the notable teachers I've ever had. Somehow, their combined influence steered me in the right direction.

Rich Maloof would like to thank:

Harvey Newquist, writing partner and friend, who gets sole credit for dreaming up this book in the first place. Whether we're in front of computers, behind guitars, or perched on barstools, it's always time well spent. Thanks for reminding me in words and by example that one really can do what one loves for a living.

Thanks to Jim Kunkel for making the guitar make sense. To Lee Knife, who patiently untangled all the crossed wires when I was learning about digital audio. To Mitch Prensky, the drummer forever keeping time in my head.

Special thanks to my wife, Kris, who withstood multiple takes of blues-rock licks at odd hours and the stream of profanities that occasionally followed. Most special thanks to our son, Daniel, who was considerate enough to postpone his debut until this book was completed. May your blue days be few.

ABOUT THE AUTHORS

HP Newquist and his writing have appeared in publications as diverse as *The New York Times, Rolling Stone, USA Today, Variety, Billboard,* and *Newsweek.* He has written a dozen books, including *Music & Technology* (Billboard Books), *The Yahoo! Ultimate Reference Guide to the Web* (HarperCollins), *The Brain Makers* (Macmillan), and *Legends of Rock Guitar* (with Pete Prown, published by Hal Leonard). His magazine work has covered topics from musicians and medicine to artificial intelligence and virtual reality. In addition, Newquist was Editor in Chief of *Guitar* magazine, and his film credits include writing the Emmy-nominated music documentary *Going Home* for the Disney Channel. He has been playing guitar since he was 15, which seems like a very long time ago.

Rich Maloof is an editor, writer, and musician based in Brooklyn, New York. He is the author of numerous instructional pieces for musicians, including the books *Joe Satriani: Riff by Riff* (Cherry Lane) and the forthcoming *Alternate Tuning Reference Guide* (Cherry Lane). Maloof served as Editor in Chief of *Guitar* magazine until 1998, when he launched his own business directing content for books, magazines, and Web sites. Among his clients to date are Berklee Press, *Billboard,* CNN, the *For Dummies* series, Musician.com, and Yahoo!, and he recently earned his first film credit as Music Consultant. He has been playing guitar for more than 25 years, ten of which were spent in a New York City band that made good music and bad money.

WHEN IT COMES TO MUSIC, WE WROTE THE BOOK.

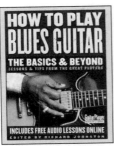

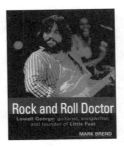
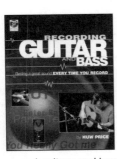
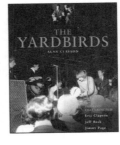

CORE-PLUS MATHEMATICS PROJECT

Course **2**
Part A

Contemporary Mathematics in Context
A Unified Approach

Arthur F. Coxford
James T. Fey
Christian R. Hirsch
Harold L. Schoen
Gail Burrill
Eric W. Hart
Ann E. Watkins
with
Mary Jo Messenger
Beth Ritsema

EVERYDAY LEARNING™

Chicago, Illinois

Cover images: Images © 1997 Photodisc, Inc.

Everyday Learning Development Staff

Editorial: Anna Belluomini, Eric Karnowski, Steve Mico

Production/Design: Fran Brown, Hector Cuadra, Norma Underwood, Marie Walz

This project was supported, in part, by the National Science Foundation.
The opinions expressed are those of the authors and not necessarily those of the Foundation.

ISBN 1-57039-485-7 (Part A)

ISBN 1-57039-489-X (Part B)

3 4 5 6 7 8 9 BP 02 01 00 99

Preface

This resource book contains blackline masters prepared to assist you as you teach Course 2, Part A, of the *Contemporary Mathematics in Context* curriculum. As you guide your students though this exciting curriculum, these resources can help you focus student attention on the important mathematics presented in each unit, help your students organize their thinking about specific problems, and save both you and your students valuable preparation time.

In general, three types of masters are included:

■ Masters to help facilitate class discussion

"Think About This Situation" transparency masters

"Checkpoint" transparency masters

Sample responses to open-ended questions

■ Masters to help students organize their responses

Generic plot grids and tables

Generic pages for the students' Math Toolkits, keyed to mathematical themes

Response templates for selected investigations

■ Masters to provide additional information or clarification

"Technology Tips" for both TI-82 and TI-83 calculators

Graphs and illustrations from the text, enlarged for easier reading

Graphs and tables supplementing the information in the text

Masters most suited for overhead projector use are labeled "Transparency Master," while those most suited to handouts (or both) are labeled "Activity Master." The *Contemporary Mathematics in Context* Teacher's Guide includes suggested uses for these masters, but it is anticipated that teachers will use these tools in many different ways compatible with their own teaching styles as well.

1. In the "Graph Models" unit in Course 1, vertex-edge graphs were shown to be useful when scheduling meeting times. For example, the Senior class at Madison High School is planning a fair to raise money for the class treasury. There are six committees and some students are on more than one committee. Committees will meet directly after school. The meeting days need to be determined and they would like to use the fewest number of days possible. Committees that share a member need to meet on different days. Below is a list of the committees and students who are on more than one committee.

Committee	Students on More Than One Committee
Food	Juan, Evelyn, Michael
Publicity	Grace, Juan
Games	Sam, Grace
Set-up/clean-up	Michael, Juan, Kelly
Raffle	Kelly, Sam
Tickets	Sam, Evelyn

   a. If you were to make a vertex-edge graph of this situation, what would the vertices of the graph represent? What would the edges of the graph represent?

   b. Draw a graph that models this situation.

   c. Color the graph using as few colors as possible.

   d. Use your coloring to answer these questions, and explain how your coloring of the graph helps you to answer each question.

   ■ Is it possible for every committee to meet once per week?

   ■ What is the fewest number of days needed to schedule all the committee meetings?

   ■ On what day should each committee meet?

The following problems could have arisen in other contexts.

2. Find an equation of the line satisfying the given conditions:

   a. With slope 5 and containing the point (3, 9)

   b. Containing the points (−2, 6) and (4, 7)

3. Solve each equation by reasoning symbolically. Check your solution. If you made an error in your symbolic reasoning, determine where your error occurred. Then explain how you should reason symbolically when solving future equations, in order to minimize the chance of repeating the same error.

a. $4(x - 2) + 6(2x - 0.5) = 5$

b. $64 = 2^t$

c. $6 - 3(4x - 1) = 18 - 3x$

d. $10P + (8P + 6) - (12P - 8) = 2P$

4. Make a sketch and then find the surface area of each of the following space-shapes.

a. A square prism with 8 cm edges on bases and 10 cm height

b. A triangular prism with a 16 cm height and a right triangle base whose right angle sides are 4 cm and 5 cm

c. A cylinder with radius of 4 cm and height of 7 cm

5. Find the slope and y-intercept of each line:

a. The line with equation

   i. $y = -3.1 + 7.8x$

   ii. $2x + 4y = 6$

b. The line with the graph shown at the right.

c. The line given by $NEXT = NOW - 4.6$, starting at 7

d. The line with the following table.

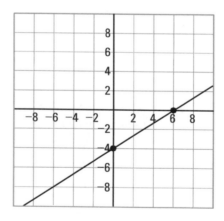

X	Y1	
-5	17	
-3	11	
-1	5	
1	-1	
3	-7	
5	-13	
7	-19	
X = -5		

Suggested Solutions

1. a. The vertices could represent the committees. An edge should be drawn if the two committees have a member in common.

b.

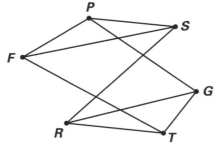

c. Responses will vary. The graph can be colored using three colors.

d. ■ Yes it is possible for each committee to meet once per week. Since only three colors are needed to color the graph, only three different meeting times are needed.

■ At least three meeting times are needed since any coloring uses at least three colors.

■ Responses will vary. One possible schedule follows.

Monday	Food and Raffle
Tuesday	Publicity and Tickets
Wednesday	Setup and Games

2. a. $y = 5x - 6$

b. $y = \frac{1}{6}x + \frac{38}{6}$

3. a. $x = 1$

b. $t = 6$

c. $x = -1$

d. $P = -3.5$

Use after page 26.

UNIT 1 • MATRIX MODELS

Suggested Solutions (*continued*)

4. a.

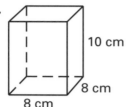

The surface area is $2(8 \times 8) + 4(8 \times 10)$ or 448 cm^2.

b.

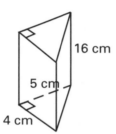

The length of the third side of the triangle is $\sqrt{16 + 25}$ or approximately 6.4.

The surface area is approximately $2\left(\frac{1}{2}\right)(4)(5) + 4(16) + 5(16) + 6.4(16)$ or 266.4 cm^2.

c.

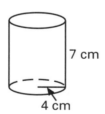

The surface area is $2(4^2 \times \pi) + 8(\pi)7$ or approximately 276.46 cm^2.

5. a. i. slope = 7.8; y-intercept = −3.1

  ii. slope = −0.5; y-intercept = 1.5

  b. slope = $\frac{2}{3}$ or 0.67; y-intercept = −4

  c. slope = −4.6; y-intercept = 7

  d. slope = −3; y-intercept = 2

Think About This Situation

Managing an athletic shoe store is a complicated job. Sales need to be tracked, inventory must be controlled carefully, and changes in the market must be anticipated. In particular, the store manager needs to know which shoes will sell. Think about the shoe store where you bought your last pair of athletic shoes.

a What information might the manager of the store want to know about the kinds of shoes the customers prefer? Make a list.

b It's not enough just to have information. The manager needs to organize and manage the information in order to make good decisions. What are some ways the manager might organize the information?

Checkpoint

ⓐ The Shoe Outlet sells women's shoes, sizes 5 to 11, and men's shoes, sizes 6 to 13. The manager would like to have an organized display of the number of pairs of shoes sold in 1996 for each shoe size. Explain how a matrix can be used to organize this data. How many rows does your matrix have? How many columns?

ⓑ What are some advantages of using matrices to organize and display data? What are some disadvantages?

ⓒ Explain how the same information can be displayed in a matrix in different ways.

Be prepared to share your group's explanations and thinking with the entire class.

Checkpoint

In the previous investigations you performed computations on the row or column entries of a matrix to get useful information about the situation being modeled. Give three examples from your analysis of pottery, shoe sales, or friendship and trust showing how you operated on the entries of the given matrix to get additional information. For each example, describe the situation, the computation, and the information obtained.

Be prepared to share your group's examples with the class.

Checkpoint

ⓐ Which of the activities about small-car production involved combining matrices by adding *corresponding entries*?

ⓑ Which of the activities about small-car production involved combining matrices by subtracting corresponding entries?

ⓒ Which of the activities about small-car production involved multiplying each entry of a matrix by a number?

ⓓ Consider all the situations you have analyzed so far. What other operations have you performed on matrices?

Be prepared to explain your group's selections to the entire class.

Think About This Situation

Have you ever switched shoe brands? Maybe you bought Reebok one year and Fila the next year.

a If you have switched athletic shoe brands, what were your reasons for switching?

b Why do you think shoe stores and shoe companies would want to know about trends in brand switching?

c How do you think they could gather information about and analyze trends in brand switching?

Entering and Multiplying Matrices

To use your calculator to multiply two matrices (for example, the brand-switching computations in activity 6 on page 29), you first need to enter the matrices into your calculator. Enter one matrix (for example, the number of buyers this year) as matrix A, and enter the other (for example, the brand-switching matrix) as B.

To do this, first access the matrix menu ([MATRX]). The third option, EDIT, allows you to enter and change the matrices stored in your calculator. Use the arrow keys to highlight this option, then select which matrix you wish to edit, for example, matrix A.

Next, you must specify how big you want this matrix to be (its dimensions). The first number is always the number of rows, and the second is the number of columns. When you have entered the dimensions of the matrix, you can fill it with the entries you need. The calculator assumes you will fill the matrix a row at a time. (See the third display below.)

After both matrices have been entered, you can multiply them from the home screen. Quit the matrix editor ([2nd] [MODE]). Now, enter the matrix names to the home screen using the NAMES menu. (See the last two displays and the keystrokes listed next to them.)

[MATRX] [▶] [▶]

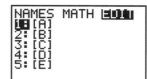

[ENTER] **1** [ENTER] **3** [ENTER]

700 [ENTER] **500** [ENTER] **400** [ENTER]

[MATRX] [▶] [▶] [▼] [ENTER]

3 [ENTER] **3** [ENTER]

.4 [ENTER] **.4** [ENTER] etc....

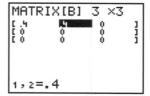

[2nd] [MODE]

[MATRX]

[ENTER] [×] [MATRX] [▼] [ENTER] [ENTER] [ENTER]

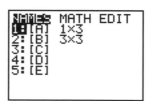

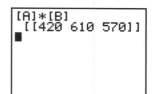

Entering and Multiplying Matrices

To use your calculator to multiply two matrices (for example, the brand-switching computations in activity 6 on page 29), you first need to enter the matrices into your calculator. Enter one matrix (for example, the number of buyers this year) as matrix A, and enter the other (for example, the brand-switching matrix) as B.

To do this, first access the matrix menu (MATRX). The third option, EDIT, allows you to enter and change the matrices stored in your calculator. Use the arrow keys to highlight this option, then select which matrix you wish to edit, for example, matrix A.

Next, you must specify how big you want this matrix to be (its dimensions). The first number is always the number of rows, and the second is the number of columns. When you have entered the dimensions of the matrix, you can fill it with the entries you need. The calculator assumes you will fill the matrix a row at a time. (See the third display below.)

After both matrices have been entered, you can multiply them from the home screen. Quit the matrix editor (2nd MODE). Now, enter the matrix names to the home screen using the NAMES menu. (See the last two displays and the keystrokes listed next to them.)

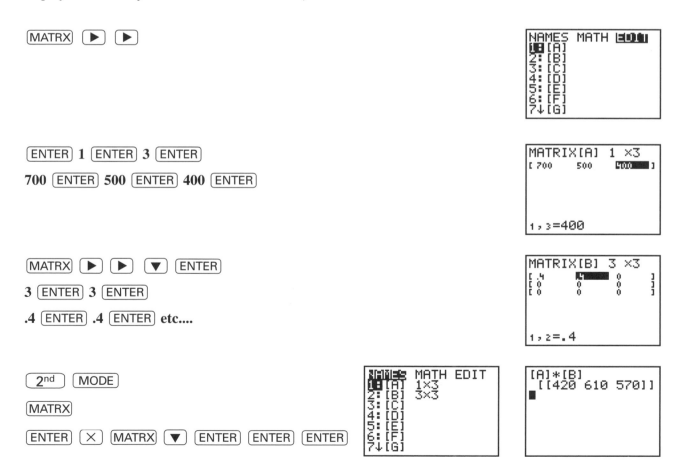

MATRX ▶ ▶

```
NAMES MATH EDIT
1:[A]
2:[B]
3:[C]
4:[D]
5:[E]
6:[F]
7↓[G]
```

ENTER 1 ENTER 3 ENTER

700 ENTER **500** ENTER **400** ENTER

```
MATRIX[A] 1 ×3
[ 700    500    400 ]


1,3=400
```

MATRX ▶ ▶ ▼ ENTER

3 ENTER 3 ENTER

.4 ENTER .4 ENTER etc....

```
MATRIX[B] 3 ×3
[.4   .4   0  ]
[0    0    0  ]
[0    0    0  ]

1,2=.4
```

2nd MODE

MATRX

ENTER × MATRX ▼ ENTER ENTER ENTER

```
NAMES MATH EDIT
1:[A]  1×3
2:[B]  3×3
3:[C]
4:[D]
5:[E]
6:[F]
7↓[G]
```

```
[A]*[B]
  [[420 610 570]]
■
```

Checkpoint

(a) Describe how to multiply a one-row matrix by another matrix. What must be true about the dimension of the other matrix?

(b) Describe any limitations you see for using the brand-switching matrix to estimate long-term shoe sales.

Be prepared to share your group's descriptions and thinking with the class.

MASTER
10

Matrix Multiplication Practice

1. Use the matrices given below to complete parts A and B.

$$A = \begin{bmatrix} 0 & 5 \end{bmatrix} \qquad B = \begin{bmatrix} 3 & 2 & 4 & 1 \end{bmatrix}$$

$$C = \begin{bmatrix} -2 \\ 0 \\ 1 \\ 0 \end{bmatrix} \qquad D = \begin{bmatrix} 2 & -1 \\ 1 & 0 \end{bmatrix}$$

$$E = \begin{bmatrix} 1 & 3 \\ 0 & -1 \\ 2 & 0 \\ -1 & 2 \end{bmatrix}$$

a. Matrix A can be multipled by which of the other matrices? Find the products.

$A \times$ _____ =

b. Matrix b can be multipled by which of the other matrices? Find the products.

$B \times$ _____ =

Checkpoint

ⓐ Describe how to multiply two matrices.

ⓑ Give two reasons why it may not make sense to multiply two particular matrices.

ⓒ Does the order of matrix multiplication matter? Explain.

ⓓ If two matrices can be multiplied, what can you say about the labels on the columns of the left matrix and the labels on the rows of the right matrix? How are the labels on the answer matrix related to the labels of the matrices being multiplied?

Be prepared to share your group's descriptions and thinking with the entire class.

Ecosystem Digraph

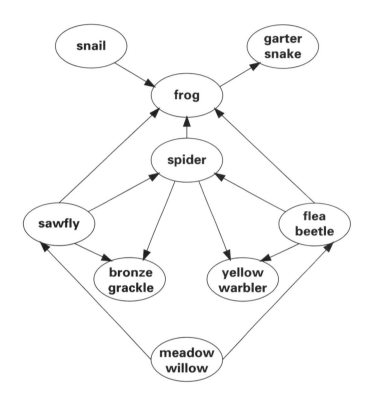

Matrices for Food Web Digraph

Adjacency matrix

	BG	FB	Fr	GS	MW	Sa	Sn	Sp	YW
Bronze Grackle	0	0	0	0	0	0	0	0	0
Flea Beetle	__	__	__	__	__	__	__	__	__
Frog	0	0	0	1	0	0	0	0	0
Garter Snake	0	0	0	0	0	0	0	0	0
Meadow Willow	0	1	0	0	0	1	0	0	0
Sawfly	1	0	1	0	0	0	0	1	0
Snail	0	0	1	0	0	0	0	0	0
Spider	1	0	__	__	0	__	0	0	1
Yellow Warbler	__	__	__	__	__	__	__	__	__

Matrix with paths of length two

	BG	FB	Fr	GS	MW	Sa	Sn	Sp	YW
Bronze Grackle	0	0	0	0	0	0	0	0	0
Flea Beetle	__	__	__	__	__	__	__	__	__
Frog	0	0	0	0	0	0	0	0	0
Garter Snake	0	0	0	0	0	0	0	0	0
Meadow Willow	1	0	2	0	__	__	__	__	__
Sawfly	1	0	1	1	0	0	0	0	1
Snail	0	0	0	1	0	0	0	0	0
Spider	0	0	0	1	0	0	0	0	0
Yellow Warbler	0	0	0	0	0	0	0	0	0

Checkpoint

a Consider paths in a digraph.

- How do paths in a food web help you track the spread of contamination through the ecosystem?

- What do paths in a tournament digraph tell you about the tournament?

b What do powers of the adjacency matrix tell you about paths in the digraph?

c Propose a general plan, using powers and sums of matrices, for ranking a tournament.

Be prepared to share your thinking and tournament-ranking plan with the class.

Checkpoint

ⓐ What are the conditions on the dimensions of two matrices that allow them to be added? Describe the dimension of the sum matrix.

ⓑ What are the conditions on the dimensions of two matrices that allow them to be multiplied? Describe the dimension of the product matrix.

ⓒ Describe and give an example of the following:
- A matrix and its opposite
- An identity matrix
- A matrix and its inverse
- A matrix that does not have an inverse

ⓓ List similarities and differences between properties of real numbers and their operations, and properties of matrices and their operations.

Be prepared to share your descriptions, examples, and thinking with the entire class.

Judge Agreements

	Ka	V	D	S	C	E	B	Ke
Kavanagh	–	76%	80%	85%	81%	88%	83%	77%
Voelker	81%	–	60%	90%	59%	86%	99%	63%
Dethmers	66%	65%	–	75%	99%	77%	72%	95%
Smith	78%	79%	63%	–	57%	81%	84%	64%
Carr	63%	58%	100%	66%	–	70%	61%	100%
Edwards	61%	68%	66%	76%	65%	–	70%	65%
Black	75%	84%	48%	77%	44%	68%	–	55%
Kelly	60%	53%	86%	63%	91%	61%	62%	–

Ally Matrix for Judges

	Ka	V	D	S	C	E	B	Ke
Kavanagh	–	__	__	__	__	__	__	__
Voelker	__	–	__	__	__	__	__	__
Dethmers	__	__	–	__	__	__	__	__
Smith	__	__	__	–	__	__	__	__
Carr	__	__	__	__	–	__	__	__
Edwards	__	__	__	__	__	–	__	__
Black	__	__	__	__	__	__	–	__
Kelly	__	__	__	__	__	__	__	–

Judge Agreements

	Ka	V	D	S	C	E	B	Ke
Kavanagh	–	76%	80%	85%	81%	88%	83%	77%
Voelker	81%	–	60%	90%	59%	86%	99%	63%
Dethmers	66%	65%	–	75%	99%	77%	72%	95%
Smith	78%	79%	63%	–	57%	81%	84%	64%
Carr	63%	58%	100%	66%	–	70%	61%	100%
Edwards	61%	68%	66%	76%	65%	–	70%	65%
Black	75%	84%	48%	77%	44%	68%	–	55%
Kelly	60%	53%	86%	63%	91%	61%	62%	–

Dominance Matrix for Judges

	Ka	V	D	S	C	E	B	Ke
Kavanagh	–	__	__	__	__	__	__	__
Voelker	__	–	__	__	__	__	__	__
Dethmers	__	__	–	__	__	__	__	__
Smith	__	__	__	–	__	__	__	__
Carr	__	__	__	__	–	__	__	__
Edwards	__	__	__	__	__	–	__	__
Black	__	__	__	__	__	__	–	__
Kelly	__	__	__	__	__	__	__	–

Think About This Situation

An expansion baseball team is planning a special promotion at its first game. Fans who arrive early will get a team athletic bag or a cap, as long as supplies last.

a Have you ever received a free promotional product at a sporting event? If so, what did you get? How much do you think it was worth? Did all the fans get something?

b For the baseball game promotion, what factors should be considered when determining how many bags and how many caps to give away?

Baseball Team Promotion

Number of Bags Given Away	Number of Caps Given Away	Total Cost of Bags and Caps Given Away	Under or Over Budget?
0	3500	$17,500	under budget
700			
1400			
2100			
2800	700	$28,700	over budget
3500			

Checkpoint

For a system of equations like the ones in this investigation:

a Describe how to represent the system with matrices.

b Describe how to solve the corresponding matrix equation $AX = C$. Explain why the method makes sense.

c Describe at least two ways to check the solution of the matrix equation that represents the system of equations.

Be prepared to share your group's descriptions and thinking with the entire class.

Baseball Team Promotion II

$b + c = 3{,}500$

b	c	Point On Graph
0	3500	(0, 3500)
500	3000	

$9b + 5c = 25{,}500$

b	c	Point On Graph
0	5100	(0, 5100)
		(500, 4200)
1000		

Checkpoint

Suppose you have a system of equations like
$4x + 10y = 1500$ and $8x + 5y = 4000$.

a What does it mean to solve the system?

b How will the solution be found on the graphs of the two equations?

c Describe how to graph the equations with and without a graphing calculator or computer software.

d In this lesson you used matrices, graphs, and tables of values to solve systems of linear equations. Describe some advantages and disadvantages of each method.

Be prepared to share your group's descriptions and thinking with the entire class.

Direct Flights

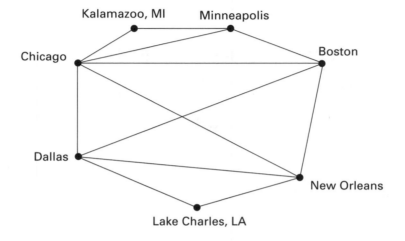

$$\begin{bmatrix} \underline{} & \underline{} & \underline{} & \underline{} & \underline{} & \underline{} & \underline{} \\ \underline{} & \underline{} & \underline{} & \underline{} & \underline{} & \underline{} & \underline{} \\ \underline{} & \underline{} & \underline{} & \underline{} & \underline{} & \underline{} & \underline{} \\ \underline{} & \underline{} & \underline{} & \underline{} & \underline{} & \underline{} & \underline{} \\ \underline{} & \underline{} & \underline{} & \underline{} & \underline{} & \underline{} & \underline{} \\ \underline{} & \underline{} & \underline{} & \underline{} & \underline{} & \underline{} & \underline{} \\ \underline{} & \underline{} & \underline{} & \underline{} & \underline{} & \underline{} & \underline{} \end{bmatrix}$$

Checkpoint

ⓐ In order for information to be useful, it must be organized.

- Describe how matrices can be used to organize information.

- Can the same information be displayed in a matrix in different ways? Explain.

- What are some advantages of using matrices to organize and display information? What are some disadvantages?

ⓑ Sometimes a situation involves two variables that are linked by two or more conditions. These situations often can be modeled by a system of two linear equations of the form $ax + by = c$. Describe at least three different methods for solving such a system of linear equations.

ⓒ List all the different operations on matrices that you have investigated in this unit.

ⓓ For each operation that you listed in part c:

- Describe how to perform the operation using paper-and-pencil.

- Describe how to perform the operation using your calculator or computer software.

- Give at least one example showing how the operation can be used to help you analyze some situation.

Be prepared to share your descriptions and examples with the entire class.

1. In the "Simulation Models" unit in Course 1, simulations were used to investigate situations that are difficult to examine more directly. For example, Denzel is taking a 10 item true-false quiz. Since he didn't study, he answers "True" or "False" at random without reading the question.

   a. Fifty trials simulating this quiz were conducted. The frequency table below shows the number of questions Denzel got correct in each trial.

Number Correct	0	1	2	3	4	5	6	7	8	9	10
Frequency	0	0	1	7	16	11	7	4	4	0	0

   Make a histogram representing these data.

   b. Without referring to the trials in part a, how many correct answers would you expect Denzel to get?

   c. Use the frequency table to estimate the number of questions Denzel will answer correctly, on average.

   d. If 70% is required to pass the quiz, estimate the probability that Denzel will pass.

The following problems could have arisen in other contexts.

2. Find the solution to each equation by reasoning with the symbolic form itself. Check your solution by substitution. If you made an error in your symbolic reasoning, determine where your error occurred. Then explain how you can minimize the chance of repeating the same error when using symbolic reasoning to solve similar equations.

   a. $4(x - 3) - 8(x - 7) = 12$

   b. $3 - 2(x + 1) - 4(2x - 6) = -8x - 1$

   c. $128\left(\frac{1}{2}\right)^t = 4$

   d. $\sqrt{P - 4} = 3$

3. Find the perimeter and area of the right triangle below.

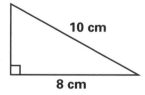

10 cm

8 cm

4. Here are two vertex-edge graphs with the vertices labeled.

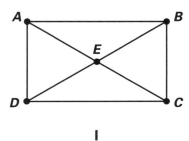

I

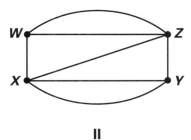

II

   a. For each graph that has an Euler path or circuit, describe it by listing the order in which the vertices are visited.

   b. Eulerize each vertex-edge graph above that does not have an Euler circuit.

5. $A = \begin{bmatrix} 2 & -1 \\ 3 & 4 \end{bmatrix}$ $B = \begin{bmatrix} -1 & -2 \\ 2 & 0 \end{bmatrix}$

   a. Find $A + B$ and $A - B$.

   b. Find $5 \cdot A$.

   c. Find $A \cdot B$ and $B \cdot A$.

6. Find the equation of each line satisfying the given conditions.

   a. With slope 5 and containing $(-2, 1)$

   b. Containing $(-2, 1)$ and $(3, -4)$

Suggested Solutions

1. a.

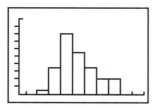

b. The theoretical number of correct answers is $0.5 \cdot 10$ or 5.

c. The average number of correct answers found using a frequency table is 4.88.

d. Denzel scored 7 or above for only 8 trials. Thus, the estimated probability is $\frac{8}{50} = 0.16$.

2. a. $x = 8$ **b.** $x = 13$

  c. $t = 5$ **d.** $P = 13$

3. The perimeter is 24 cm. The area is 24 cm^2.

4. a. Graph I has neither an Euler path nor an Euler circuit. Graph II has an Euler path. An Euler path will start at either W or Y and end at the other. One path is $W - Z - W - X - Z - Y - X - Y$.

  b. One possible Eulerization of each graph is shown here.

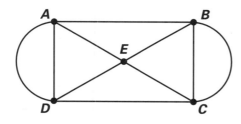
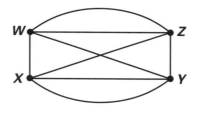

5. a. $A + B = \begin{bmatrix} 1 & -3 \\ 5 & 4 \end{bmatrix}$ $A - B = \begin{bmatrix} 3 & 1 \\ 1 & 4 \end{bmatrix}$

  b. $5 \cdot A = \begin{bmatrix} 10 & -5 \\ 15 & 20 \end{bmatrix}$

  c. $A \cdot B = \begin{bmatrix} -4 & -4 \\ 5 & -6 \end{bmatrix}$ $B \cdot A = \begin{bmatrix} -8 & -7 \\ 4 & -2 \end{bmatrix}$

6. a. $y = 5x + 11$

  b. $y = -x - 1$

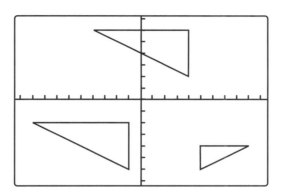

Think About This Situation

Examine the calculator graphics display above.

a How do you think such graphics displays are produced?

b How could you describe the locations of the three triangles?

c Describe how you could transform the *leftmost* triangle so that it will coincide with the *upper* triangle.

d Describe how you might transform the *rightmost* triangle so that it will coincide with the *leftmost* triangle.

Checkpoint

ⓐ Write a formula for calculating the distance, D, between any two points $P(x_1, y_1)$ and $Q(x_2, y_2)$.

$D =$ _____

ⓑ Explain in words how this formula determines the distance.

Be prepared to explain your formula and why it works to the entire class.

Distance Algorithm

Step 1: Get the coordinates of one point.
Step 2: Get the coordinates of the other point. $\Big\}$input
Step 3: Use the coordinates and the distance
formula to compute the desired distance. $\Big\}$processing
Step 4: Display and label the distance. $\}$output

Distance Program

DIST Program	**Function in Program**
ClrHome	Clears display screen
Input "X COORD",A	
Input "Y COORD",B	Enters inputs
Input "X COORD",C	
Input "Y COORD",D	
$\sqrt{((A - C)^2 + (B - D)^2)} \to L$	Calculates distance and stores value in memory location L
Disp "DISTANCE IS",L	Outputs calculated distance with label

Checkpoint

ⓐ Suppose $P(x_1, y_1)$ and $Q(x_2, y_2)$ are two points. Write a formula for the midpoint of segment PQ. Explain why this formula makes sense.

ⓑ Describe the importance of the input, processing, and output parts of the algorithms developed in this investigation.

ⓒ Describe an algorithm that could be used to write a program that would draw a segment on a graphics screen.

Be prepared to explain your formula, algorithm, and thinking to the class.

Checkpoint

ⓐ Suppose a line l in a coordinate plane has slope $\frac{p}{q}$.

- What is the slope of a line parallel to l? Why must this be the case?

- What is the slope of a line perpendicular to l? Why does this seem reasonable?

ⓑ Given quadrilateral $QUAD$ with vertex matrix

$$QUAD = \begin{bmatrix} -6 & 6 & 0 & -12 \\ -3 & 3 & -15 & 9 \end{bmatrix},$$

determine specifically what shape $QUAD$ is. Explain how you can be sure.

Be prepared to discuss your ideas with the class.

**MASTER
31**

Coordinate Models I

Geometric Idea	Coordinate Model	Example
Point	Ordered pair (x, y) of real numbers	_____
Plane	All possible ordered pairs (x, y) of real numbers	(No example needed.)
Line	All ordered pairs (x, y) satisfying $y = a + bx$ or $x = c$	$y = -4 + 2x$
Parallel lines	_____	_____
Perpendicular lines	_____	_____
Distance	_____	_____
Midpoint	_____	_____

Beginning Programming

After you have thought through an algorithm that will perform the actions you want the calculator to do, you need to translate these steps into calculator instructions. This is programming. This tip guides you through entering, into your calculator, the DIST Program that is in Investigation 1 (page 85) of your textbook.

a. Access the PRGM menu and select NEW. This permits you to write a new program. Press ENTER (or 1) and name the program DIST by typing in these letters. Press ENTER when finished.

b. In order to make your program work, you need a way to let the user enter the coordinates of the two points. To accomplish this, press PRGM and select the I/O (Input/Output) menu. Press ENTER and the word "Input" will appear in the first line of your program.

c. To make the program user-friendly, tell the user what to input by typing "**X⊔COORD⊔**". (The quotation marks let the calculator know that everything between them is to be displayed.) Then tell the calculator where to store the inputted data by typing **A**. (See the display screen shown here.) To type a letter at this stage of the program, press ALPHA and the key below that letter (in this case, MATH). Set A-LOCK when typing several letters. Press ENTER after typing the line. Do not worry if the command takes more than one line. Note the space (produced by pressing ALPHA 0) between some characters in the screen display at the right.

```
PROGRAM:DIST
:Input "X COORD"
,A
:█
```

d. Continue in this manner, calling up the I/O menu each time to get the Input command. Remember to press ENTER after each line is completed. The second, third, and fourth lines of your program should read

> :Input "Y⊔COORD⊔", B
>
> :Input "X⊔COORD⊔", C
>
> :Input "Y⊔COORD⊔", D

What is the relationship between the variables *A*, *B*, *C,* and *D* in your program and the variables in your distance formula?

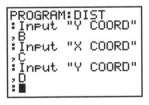

```
PROGRAM:DIST
:Input "Y COORD"
,B
:Input "X COORD"
,C
:Input "Y COORD"
,D
:█
```

e. Now you are ready to type in the most important line of the program—the one that does the computation. To do this, enter the expression for computing distance from the distance formula and then store the resulting value in calculator memory location L (for length). To do this, type:

$$\sqrt{((A - C)^2 + (B - D)^2)} \quad \boxed{STO \blacktriangleright} \quad L \quad \boxed{ENTER}$$

f. To display the calculated distance, access the I/O menu and select Disp. Now type: "**DISTANCE␣IS␣**", **L** and then press $\boxed{ENTER}$.

g. End your program by pressing $\boxed{2^{nd}}$ QUIT.

h. Check your program for errors by running it. This is done by pressing $\boxed{PRGM}$, choosing DIST from the menu, and pressing $\boxed{ENTER}$. Enter several pairs of points to see whether or not your program computes the correct distance. If the program is not calculating distances correctly, check it to be sure you typed it in properly. (For a program you write yourself, you may have to look more closely at what the instructions are meant to do.) This process of checking and fixing a program is called "debugging".

Beginning Programming

After you have thought through an algorithm that will perform the actions you want the calculator to do, you need to translate these steps into calculator instructions. This is programming. This tip guides you through entering, into your calculator, the DIST Program that is in Investigation 1 (page 85) of your textbook.

a. Access the PRGM menu and select NEW. This permits you to write a new program. Press [ENTER] (or 1) and name the program DIST by typing in these letters. Press [ENTER] when finished.

b. In order to make your program work, you need a way to let the user enter the coordinates of the two points. To accomplish this, press [PRGM] and select the I/O (Input/Output) menu. Press [ENTER] and the word "Input" will appear in the first line of your program.

c. To make the program user-friendly, tell the user what to input by typing "**X␣COORD␣**". (The quotation marks let the calculator know that everything between them is to be displayed.) Then tell the calculator where to store the inputted data by typing a comma and then **A**. (See the display screen shown here.) To type a letter at this stage of the program, press [ALPHA] and the key below that letter, in this case, [MATH]. Set A-LOCK when typing several letters. Press [ENTER] after typing the line. Do not worry if the command takes more than one line. Note the space (produced by pressing [ALPHA] 0) between some characters in the screen display at the right.

```
PROGRAM:DIST
:Input "X COORD"
,A
:■
```

d. Continue in this manner, calling up the I/O menu each time to get the Input command. Remember to press [ENTER] after each line is completed. The second, third, and fourth lines of your program should read

:Input "Y␣COORD␣", B

:Input "X␣COORD␣", C

:Input "Y␣COORD␣", D

What is the relationship between the variables *A*, *B*, *C* and *D* in your program and the variables in your distance formula?

```
PROGRAM:DIST
:Input "Y COORD"
,B
:Input "X COORD"
,C
:Input "Y COORD"
,D
:■
```

e. Now you are ready to type in the most important line of the program—the one that does the computation. To do this, enter the expression for computing distance from the distance formula and then store the resulting value in calculator memory location L (for length). To do this, type:

$$\sqrt{((A - C)^2 + (B - D)^2)} \quad \boxed{\text{STO▶}} \quad \textbf{L} \quad \boxed{\text{ENTER}}$$

f. To display the calculated distance, access the I/O menu and select Disp. Now type: **"DISTANCE␣IS␣"**, **L** and then press $\boxed{\text{ENTER}}$.

g. End your program by pressing $\boxed{\text{2}^{\text{nd}}}$ QUIT.

h. Check your program for errors by running it. This is done by pressing $\boxed{\text{PRGM}}$, choosing DIST from the menu, and pressing $\boxed{\text{ENTER}}$. Enter several pairs of points to see whether or not your program computes the correct distance. If the program is not calculating distances correctly, check it to be sure you typed it in properly. (For a program you write yourself, you may have to look more closely at what the instructions are meant to do.) This process of checking and fixing a program is called "debugging".

**MASTER
34a**

Plotting Points and Drawing Line Segments

These two activites will help you learn how to plot points and draw line segments on your calculator.

1. a. Begin by clearing all $\boxed{\text{Y=}}$ functions from your graphing calculator. Check that all STAT PLOTS are turned off.

b. Access the $\boxed{\text{WINDOW}}$ menu. Set your values as shown at the right.

- Explain the purpose of the $\boxed{\text{WINDOW}}$ and the meaning of variables Xmin, Xmax, Xscl, Ymin, Ymax, and Yscl.

- If someone graphed a point and it appeared in this window, what would you know about its coordinates?

c. Next, select FORMAT from the $\boxed{\text{WINDOW}}$ menu. Select CoordOn, press $\boxed{\text{GRAPH}}$, and then press any one of the four arrow keys.

- What do you notice about the coordinates of the cursor as you move it?

- What happens if you select CoordOff?

d. Access the WINDOW-FORMAT menu again. Select GridOn, then press $\boxed{\text{GRAPH}}$. What happens? Do you prefer GridOn or GridOff?

e. Continue to experiment with the WINDOW-FORMAT menu. Try using AxesOn then AxesOff, and LabelOff then LabelOn. Which overall format do you prefer?

f. Select the $\boxed{\text{ZOOM}}$ menu and choose ZInteger (choice 8) and then press $\boxed{\text{ENTER}}$ when the graphing screen appears. Press any of the arrow keys.

- What do you notice about the coordinates of the cursor as you move it?

- What is your viewing window now?

g. Select the $\boxed{\text{ZOOM}}$ menu and choose ZDecimal (choice 4). Press any of the arrow keys.

- What do you notice about the coordinates of the cursor as you move it?

- What is your viewing window now?

2. a. The first step in producing a shape is to display individual points. In this activity you will explore how the TI-82 graphing calculator can display individual points in a coordinate plane. Check that GridOff is selected from the WINDOW-FORMAT menu. Press [2nd] QUIT to return to the home screen. Select POINTS from the DRAW menu. Choose Pt-On (. Complete the command with **3, 2)** and press [ENTER]. What do you notice in the first quadrant?

b. You also can plot points from the graphics display. Use the DRAW-POINTS menu to choose Pt-On(again. This time, after you press [ENTER], you will go immediately to the display of the coordinate plane. Using the arrow keys, move the cursor to any point you choose, then press [ENTER] to plot the point. Display additional points in the plane by moving the cursor and pressing [ENTER].

c. Other choices you may need on the DRAW-POINTS menu are Pt-Off(and Pt-Change(. Experiment with ways to use these commands.

d. To draw a line segment from the home screen, select Line(from the DRAW menu. Complete the command; for example, type **3, 2, -1, -2)** and press [ENTER]. You should see a line segment that has endpoints (3, 2) and (−1, −2).

e. You also can draw line segments from the graphics display. Select Line(from the DRAW menu. Then use the arrow keys to move the cursor to one endpoint of your desired segment and press [ENTER]. Move the cursor to the other endpoint and press [ENTER]. You should see the desired line segment.

f. To clear your graphics display, access the DRAW menu and select ClrDraw.

Plotting Points and Drawing Line Segments

These two activites will help you learn how to plot points and draw line segments on your calculator.

1. a. Begin by clearing all ⬭Y=⬭ functions from your graphing calculator. Check that all STAT PLOTS are turned off.

b. Access the ⬭WINDOW⬭ menu. Set your values as shown at the right.

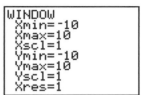

- Explain the purpose of the ⬭WINDOW⬭ and the meaning of variables Xmin, Xmax, Xscl, Ymin, Ymax, and Yscl.

- If someone graphed a point and it appeared in this window, what would you know about its coordinates?

c. Next, select FORMAT (⬭2nd⬭ ⬭ZOOM⬭). Select CoordOn, press ⬭GRAPH⬭, and then press any one of the four arrow keys.

- What do you notice about the coordinates of the cursor as you move it?

- What happens if you select CoordOff?

d. Access the FORMAT menu again. Select GridOn, then press ⬭GRAPH⬭. What happens? Do you prefer GridOn or GridOff?

e. Continue to experiment with the FORMAT menu. Try using AxesOn then AxesOff, and LabelOff then LabelOn. Which overall format do you prefer?

f. Select the ⬭ZOOM⬭ menu and choose ZInteger (choice 8) and then press ⬭ENTER⬭ when the graphing screen appears. Press any of the arrow keys.

- What do you notice about the coordinates of the cursor as you move it?

- What is your viewing window now?

g. Select the ⬭ZOOM⬭ menu and choose ZDecimal (choice 4). Press any of the arrow keys.

- What do you notice about the coordinates of the cursor as you move it?

- What is your viewing window now?

2. a. The first step in producing a shape is to display individual points. In this activity you will explore how the TI-83 graphing calculator can display individual points in a coordinate plane. Check that GridOff is selected from the FORMAT menu. Press [2nd] QUIT to return to the home screen. Select POINTS from the DRAW menu. Choose Pt-On(. Complete the command with **3, 2)** and press [ENTER]. What do you notice in the first quadrant?

   b. You also can plot points from the graphics display. Use the DRAW-POINTS menu to choose Pt-On(again. This time, after you press [ENTER], you will go immediately to the display of the coordinate plane. Using the arrow keys, move the cursor to any point you choose, then press [ENTER] to plot the point. Display additional points in the plane by moving the cursor and pressing [ENTER].

   c. Other choices you may need on the DRAW-POINTS menu are Pt-Off(and Pt-Change(. Experiment with ways to use these commands.

   d. To draw a line segment from the home screen, select Line(from the DRAW menu. Complete the command; for example, type **3, 2, -1, -2)** and press [ENTER]. You should see a line segment that has endpoints (3, 2) and (–1, –2).

   e. You also can draw line segments from the graphics display. Select Line(from the DRAW menu. Then use the arrow keys to move the cursor to one endpoint of your desired segment and press [ENTER]. Move the cursor to the other endpoint and press [ENTER]. You should see the desired line segment.

   f. To clear your graphics display, access the DRAW menu and select ClrDraw.

Families of Lines

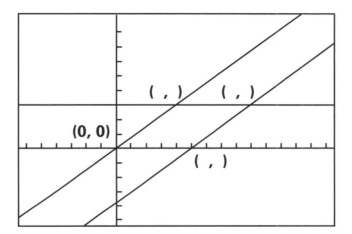

Checkpoint

You now have added a linear-combination method to your tool kit for solving systems of linear equations. Look back at the geometry and the algebra of this method.

ⓐ Describe how you can predict whether or not a system of linear equations has a solution by examining the equations themselves.

ⓑ How is the graph of a linear equation related to the graph of a nonzero multiple of that equation?

ⓒ What is true about the graph of a linear combination of two linear equations if the original lines intersect? If the lines are parallel?

ⓓ How can you find the solution to a system of linear equations by using a linear combination of the equations?

ⓔ Describe five ways to check a solution to a system of linear equations, when the solution was found by a linear-combination method.

Be prepared to explain your ideas to the entire class.

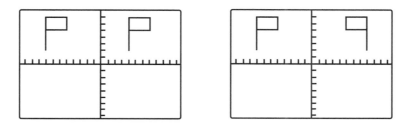

Think About This Situation

The calculator screens above show two flag patterns. The scale on both axes is 1.

a Examine the first display.

- What single transformation will map the left flag onto the right flag?

- How do you think coordinates might be used to create the appearance of moving the left flag to the position of the right flag?

- Suppose you want to produce a flag in each of the remaining quadrants so that the resulting flag patterns will have the *x*-axis as a line of symmetry. What steps would a calculator program need to follow in order to do this?

b Now examine the second display.

- Suppose you want to produce a flag in each of the remaining quadrants so that the resulting flag pattern is symmetric with respect to both the *x*-axis and the *y*-axis. What steps would a calculator program need to follow in order to do this?

- Will this pattern have any other symmetry? Explain.

TRANSL Program	Comments
Input "X⎵COORD-PRE⎵", A	Requests input for *x*-coordinate of the initial point. Stores the value in variable named A.
Input "Y⎵COORD-PRE⎵", B	_____
Input "X⎵COMP-TRANS⎵", H	_____
Input "Y⎵COMP-TRANS⎵", K	Requests input for *y*-component of translation. Stores value in variable named K.
ClrDraw	Clears all drawings.
Pt-On (A, B)	Illuminates point with coordinates (A, B).
Pt-On (A + H, B + K)	_____
Pause	Stops a program from continuing until ⟨ENTER⟩ is pressed.
Disp "PRE-IMAGE"	Displays word PRE-IMAGE.
Disp A, B	_____
Disp "IMAGE"	_____
Disp A + H, B + K	_____

Checkpoint

You now have developed coordinate models for translations and certain line reflections.

a How do the rules relating coordinates for line reflections differ from the rules for translations?

b How do the rules for reflecting across the lines $y = x$ and $y = -x$ differ from rules for reflecting across an axis?

c Suppose the reflection image of a point A across a line m is A'. Describe how segment AA' and m are related.

Be prepared to explain your group's ideas to the class.

Rotation Images

Pre-image	90° Counterclockwise Rotation Image	180° Counterclockwise Rotation Image	270° Counterclockwise Rotation Image
A (0, 0)	A' (,)		
B (3, 3)	B' (,)		
C (5, 5)	C' (,)		
D (7, 3)	D' (,)		
E (5, 1)	E' (,)		
(–2, –5)			
(–4, 1)			
(5, –3)			

Checkpoint

Summarize the coordinate patterns for each rotation about the origin.

a For a rotation of 90° counterclockwise: $(x, y) \rightarrow (\_ , \_)$

b For a rotation of 180° counterclockwise: $(x, y) \rightarrow (\_ , \_)$

c For a rotation of 270° counterclockwise: $(x, y) \rightarrow (\_ , \_)$

d For a rotation of 270° clockwise: $(x, y) \rightarrow (\_ , \_)$

Be prepared to explain your coordinate patterns to the entire class.

MASTER 43

Coordinate Models II

Geometric Idea	Coordinate Model	Example
Translation	$(x, y) \rightarrow (x + h, y + k)$	
Reflection across x-axis	$(x, y) \rightarrow (\ \ ,\ \ )$	
Reflection across y-axis	$(x, y) \rightarrow (\ \ ,\ \ )$	
Reflection across line $y = x$		
Reflection across line $y = -x$		
90° counterclockwise rotation		
180° rotation		
270° counterclockwise rotation		$(2, 5) \rightarrow (5, -2)$

Size Transformation of Magnitude 3

Pre-Image   Image

(x, y) $\rightarrow$ $(3x, 3y)$

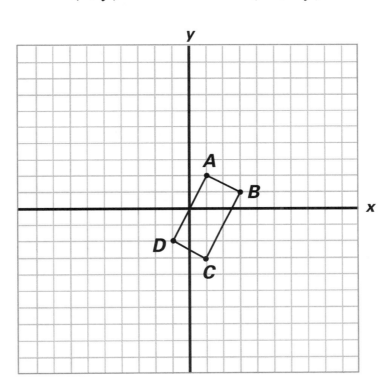

Checkpoint

ⓐ Explain why the transformation in activity 1 is or is not a size transformation.

ⓑ Suppose a size transformation with magnitude k and center at the origin O maps A onto A', B onto B', and C onto C'.

- How is the distance $A'B'$ related to the distance AB?

- If $\triangle ABC$ has an area of 25 square units, what is the area of $\triangle A'B'C'$?

- How is distance OC' related to distance OC?

- Where do lines AA' and CC' intersect? Does BB' intersect there too?

Be prepared to explain your conclusions to the entire class.

Size Transformation with Magnitude $k > 1$

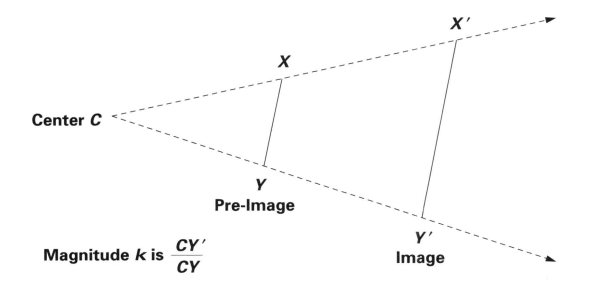

Center C

X'

X

Y

Pre-Image

Y'

Image

Magnitude k is $\dfrac{CY'}{CY}$

Checkpoint

Suppose a shape S' is the image of a shape S under a size transformation of magnitude k.

a Make a list of properties of S that are also properties of S'.

b How are corresponding distances in S and S' related?

c If S has area 35 cm^2, then what is the area of S'?

d How could you find the center of the size transformation?

e If the size transformation has center C and X' is the image of X, how could you find the magnitude k?

Be prepared to share your conclusions and reasoning with the entire class.

Checkpoint

a What kind of transformation is formed by composing the transformations given in each case below? Be as specific as you can.

- Two translations

- Two rotations (of any degree) about the origin

- Two size transformations with center at the origin

- Two line reflections

b For each pair of transformations given above, suppose a 5-cm segment is transformed by the composition. What can you say about the segment and its image? Consider such characteristics as parallelism, length, and so on.

Be prepared to share your group's thinking with the class.

Checkpoint

a Refer to this coordinate grid. The scale on both axes is 1. For each pair of triangles, determine if they are similar. If so, describe a similarity transformation that will map the first onto the second.

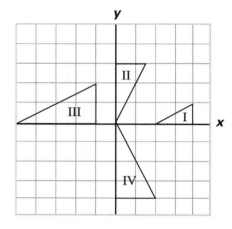

- △I and △III

- △II and △IV

- △IV and △I

b How do similarity transformations affect areas of shapes? How would you convince others of your conclusion?

Be prepared to share your descriptions and conclusions with the entire class.

Checkpoint

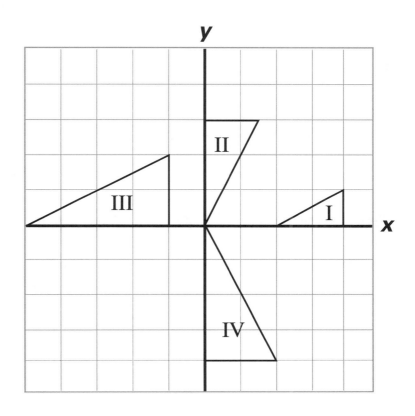

Think About This Situation

Analyze the "Flag Drill" animation produced by the GEOXPLOR program, or an animation produced by other software.

a Describe all the different transformations that appear to be involved in the animation.

b How do you think the animation is accomplished?

c Describe some examples of other computer animations that you have seen.

FLAGTURN Program

Comments

ClrDraw	Clears all drawings.
For(N,1,8,1)	Beginning of loop. Transforms the flag in 8 steps.
[A]*[B] → [B]	Stores the product of the transformation matrix A and matrix B in matrix B.
Line ([B](1,1),[B](2,1),[B](1,2),[B](2,2))	Draws a line segment from the point whose coordinates are in the 1st column of the shape matrix B to the point whose coordinates are in the 2nd column of B.
Line ([B](1,2),[B](2,2),[B](1,3),[B](2,3))	Draws a line segment from the point whose coordinates are in the 2nd column of B to the point whose coordinates are in the 3rd column of B.
Line ([B](1,3),[B](2,3),[B](1,4),[B](2,4))	Draws a line segment from the 3rd column point to the 4th column point.
For(K,1,25,1)	Beginning of pause loop. This loop causes the program to wait a moment before changing the drawing.
End	End of pause loop.
ClrDraw	Clears all drawings.
End	End of loop (N, 1, 8, 1).
Stop	End of program.

Checkpoint

a Explain how to use the coordinate representation of a 90° clockwise rotation about the origin to find the matrix representation for that rotation. Find the matrix.

b Describe how to change the Flag Turn Algorithm to rotate the flag clockwise about the origin using steps of 90°.

c Describe how matrices can be used to create an animation of a flag spinning around the origin.

Be prepared to share your group's matrix and descriptions with the class.

Checkpoint

ⓐ Explain how to use the coordinate rule for a transformation to find the matrix representation of the transformation.

ⓑ Write the matrix that represents a size transformation of magnitude k.

ⓒ Explain how your matrix in part b can be used to find the image of a point and the image of a polygon.

Be prepared to explain your matrix and methods to the entire class.

Checkpoint

ⓐ Describe several different ways that coordinates are used to model geometric ideas. Illustrate with examples.

ⓑ Describe how to solve a system of two linear equations using a linear-combination method. How can this method be interpreted geometrically? Illustrate with an example.

ⓒ Describe several different ways that matrices are used to model geometric ideas. Illustrate with examples.

ⓓ How do rigid transformations affect distance? Angle measure? Parallelism of lines? Areas of plane shapes?

ⓔ How do size transformations affect distance? Angle measure? Parallelism of lines? Areas of plane shapes? Distances of a point and its image from the center of the transformation?

ⓕ Describe how animation effects can be produced by a graphing calculator.

Be prepared to share your descriptions, illustrations, and summaries with the class.

1. Suppose you set up an experiment in which you toss 216 dice. You remove all dice that show six, then toss the remaining dice. Once again, remove the dice that show six, and then continue this process.

   a. What equation would best model the number of dice remaining after the xth toss and removal?

   b. Approximately how many dice would you expect to be left after two repetitions of the toss-remove experiment?

2. Solve each system of equations by reasoning with the symbolic forms themselves. Check your solution by substitution. If you made an error in your symbolic reasoning, determine where your error occurred. Then explain how you could minimize the chance of repeating the same error when using symbolic reasoning to solve similar systems.

   a. $5x + 20y = 1000$

   $3x + 2y = 120$

   b. $5x + 6y = 18$

   $-5x + 7y = 21$

3. Find an equation to represent each table or graph below.

   a.

X	Y1	
-2	8	
-1	5	
0	2	
1	-1	
2	-4	
3	-7	
4	-10	

   X= -2

   b.

X	Y1	
0	5	
1	15	
2	45	
3	135	
4	405	
5	1215	
6	3645	

   X= 0

   c.

   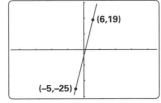

   (6,19)

   (−5,−25)

   d.

X	Y1	
0	1	
1	.25	
2	.0625	
3	.01563	
4	.00391	
5	9.8E −4	
6	2.4E −4	

   X= 0

4. The equations of the two lines on the diagram shown here are
$4x + 3y = 12$ and $-x + 6y = 6$.

   a. Label each line with the equation that
   corresponds to it.

   b. Find the coordinates of the point of
   intersection of these lines.

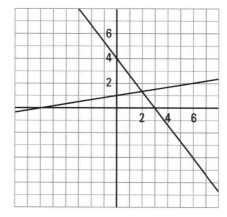

5. In the "Patterns of Location, Shape, and Size" unit, you investigated coordinate models of geometric objects. For example, suppose you have a triangle with vertices at the points $A(1, 2)$, $B(4, 1)$, and $C(6, 7)$.

   a. On a coordinate system, sketch $\triangle ABC$. Give the matrix representation of the same triangle.

   b. Find the midpoints of sides AB and BC. Call them D and E.

   c. Determine as specifically as possible what special kind of triangle ABC is. Explain your reasoning.

   d. Find the equations of the lines CD and AE.

6. Write each of the following expressions in shorter form using exponents.

   a. $-4 \times -4 \times -4 \times -4 =$

   b. $(1.7) \times (1.7) \times (1.7) \times a \times a =$

7. Suppose $P = 8(2)^k$ and $A = -3B + 5$.

   a. Find the value of P if $k = 3$.

   b. Find the value of k if $P = 256$.

   c. Find the value of A if $B = -4$.

   d. Find the value of B if $A = -10$.

8. Calculate the value of each expression below.

   a. $-3 \times (2 + 3)^2 + 1$

   b. 4.3×10^{-5}

Suggested Solutions

1. a. $y = 216 \left(\frac{5}{6}\right)^x$ **b.** 150 dice remain

2. a. $x = 8,\ y = 48$ **b.** $x = 0,\ y = 3$

3. a. $y = -3x + 2$ **b.** $y = 5(3)^x$

   c. $y = 4x - 5$ **d.** $y = (0.25)^x$

4. a.   **b.** $(2,\ 1\frac{1}{3})$

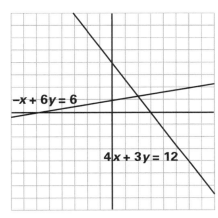

5. a. $\triangle ABC = \begin{bmatrix} 1 & 4 & 6 \\ 2 & 1 & 7 \end{bmatrix}$

b. Midpoint of $AB = D\left(\frac{5}{2},\ \frac{3}{2}\right)$; midpoint of $BC = E(5,\ 4)$

c. $\triangle ABC$ is a right triangle since the slope of line AB is $-\frac{1}{3}$ and the slope of line BC is $\frac{6}{2}$ or 3. Since the slopes are negative reciprocals, the lines are perpendicular.

d. Equation of line CD: $7y - 11x = -17$

                                 $y = \frac{11}{7}x - \frac{17}{7}$

    Equation of line AE: $2y - x = 3$

                                   $y = \frac{1}{2}x + \frac{3}{2}$

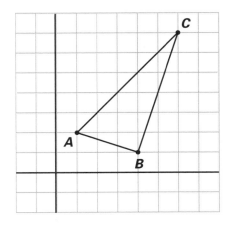

6. a. $(-4)^4$ **b.** $(1.7)^3 a^2$

7. a. $P = 64$ **b.** $k = 5$

   c. $A = 17$ **d.** $B = 5$

8. a. -74 **b.** 0.000043

Think About This Situation

a Describe how you would display or summarize the data to help you answer the question: Does there appear to be an association between the *education expenditure per student* and the *overall score*?

b How might you measure the *strength* of association?

c Do you think the value of one of the two variables causes or otherwise influences the value of the other?

d UCLA, which was rated among the top 50 universities in the United States, has an expenditure of $21,500 per student. How might you predict the overall score of UCLA? How much confidence would you have in this prediction?

MASTER 57

Music Rankings Scatterplot

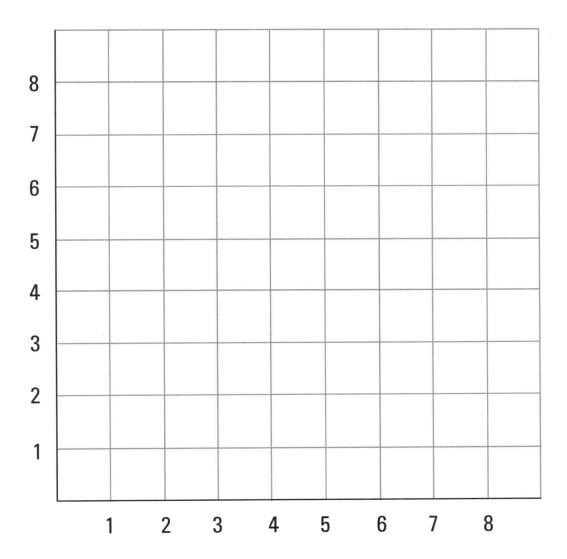

Students: _____

_____

Correlation: r_s = _____

Checkpoint

a Sketch a scatterplot showing a strong positive association for paired rankings. Give an example of two variables that aren't ranks but might have a scatterplot that looks like yours.

b Sketch a scatterplot showing a strong negative association for paired rankings. Give an example of two variables that aren't ranks but might have a scatterplot that looks like yours.

c Describe your method for assigning a numerical measure to the strength of the association seen in a scatterplot of rankings. How does your numerical measure distinguish between positive association and negative association?

Be prepared to explain your sketches and the method you invented to the class.

Music Rankings Table

Type of Music	Your Ranking	Partner's Ranking	Difference of Rankings (d)	Squared Difference (d^2)
Alternative Rock				
Classical				
Country				
Easy Listening				
Hip-Hop				
Jazz				
Latino				
Rhythm and Blues				
$n = 8$				$\sum d^2 =$

Rankings of Metropolitan Areas

Metro Area	Population	Crime	Health Care	Education
Los Angeles, CA	1	14	2	4
New York, NY	2	15	1	2
Chicago, IL	3	13	3	3
Philadelphia, PA	4	4	4	8
Washington, DC	5	5	5	7
Detroit, MI	6	9	7	9
Houston, TX	7	7	6	15
Atlanta, GA	8	10	11	14
Boston, MA	9	6	10	1
Riverside, CA	10	11	15	13
Dallas, TX	11	12	14	11
San Diego, CA	12	8	13	12
Minneapolis, MN	13	2	8	10
Orange County, CA	14	3	12	5
Long Island, NY	15	1	9	6

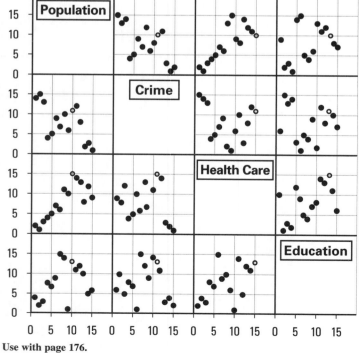

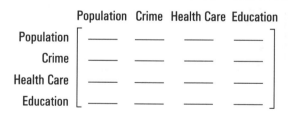

Checkpoint

a How can positive rank correlation be seen in a list of paired rankings? In a scatterplot? In the value of r_s?

b How can negative rank correlation be seen in a list of paired rankings? In a scatterplot? In the value of r_s?

c What information can you get from a scatterplot matrix that is difficult to see in the table of data?

Be prepared to explain your thinking to the entire class.

Causes of Injuries in the United States

Product	Number of Injuries, 1992 (Estimated)	Rank
Bathtubs and Showers	150,995	7
Bicycles and Accessories	649,536	2
Chairs	307,800	5
Drinking Glasses	130,201	9
Fences and Fence Posts	123,014	10
Knives	468,644	3
Ladders	139,595	8
Nails, Screws, and Tacks	239,711	6
Stairs and Steps	1,058,787	1
Tables	346,874	4

Source: *The Universal Almanac, 1994.* New York: Andrews and McMeel, 1993.

Think about This Situation

Examine the scatterplot matrix of chicken fast-food entrees.

a The strongest positive association appears to be between what pair of variables?

b How might you compute a measure of the strength of the association between sodium (salt) in milligrams and total calories?

c Does an increase in sodium cause an increase in calories? Explain your thinking.

Finding Pearson's Correlation Coefficient

x	y	$x-\bar{x}$	$(x-\bar{x})^2$	$y-\bar{y}$	$(y-\bar{y})^2$	$(x-\bar{x})(y-\bar{y})$
1	2					
2	4					
3	6					
Sum (Σ)						

x	y	$x-\bar{x}$	$(x-\bar{x})^2$	$y-\bar{y}$	$(y-\bar{y})^2$	$(x-\bar{x})(y-\bar{y})$
1	10					
3	8					
5	3					
7	3					
Sum (Σ)						

Finding the Correlation Coefficient

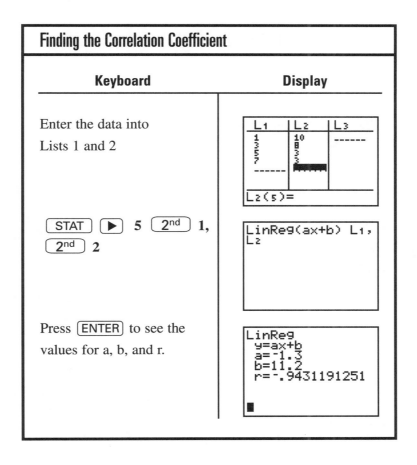

Finding the Correlation Coefficient

Keyboard	Display
Enter the data into Lists 1 and 2	L1, L2, L3 table; L2(5)=
[STAT] [▶] 5 [2nd] 1, [2nd] 2	LinReg(ax+b) L1, L2
Press [ENTER] to see the values for a, b, and r.	LinReg y=ax+b a=⁻1.3 b=11.2 r=⁻.9431191251

Finding the Correlation Coefficient

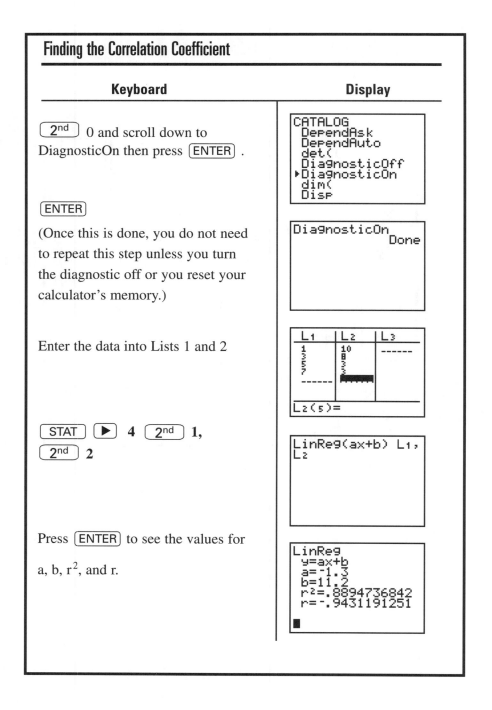

Finding the Correlation Coefficient

Keyboard	Display
2nd 0 and scroll down to DiagnosticOn then press ENTER .	CATALOG DependAsk DependAuto det(DiagnosticOff ▶DiagnosticOn dim(Disp
ENTER (Once this is done, you do not need to repeat this step unless you turn the diagnostic off or you reset your calculator's memory.)	DiagnosticOn Done
Enter the data into Lists 1 and 2	L₁ L₂ L₃ 1 10 3 8 7 3 ------ ------ L₂(5)=
STAT ▶ 4 2nd 1, 2nd 2	LinReg(ax+b) L₁, L₂
Press ENTER to see the values for a, b, r^2, and r.	LinReg y=ax+b a=-1.3 b=11.2 r^2=.8894736842 r=-.9431191251

Checkpoint

ⓐ Describe how to use Pearson's formula for a correlation coefficient.

ⓑ If the correlation coefficient is 1, what does that tell you about the points on the scatterplot? If the correlation coefficient is −1, what does that tell you?

ⓒ For what kinds of data is it appropriate to compute Pearson's correlation coefficient?

Be prepared to share your description and thinking with the class.

Checkpoint

ⓐ Explain why it is important to examine a scatterplot of a set of data even though you have found the correlation coefficient.

ⓑ For each of the plots below, identify and describe the effect of the influential point on the correlation coefficient.

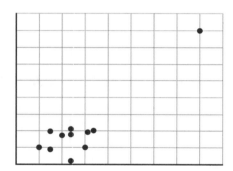 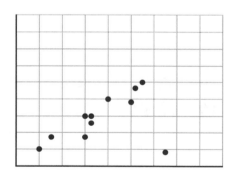

ⓒ Does a high correlation indicate a linear relationship? Does a low correlation indicate that the relationship is not linear?

Be prepared to defend your views to your classmates.

Checkpoint

There are several reasons why variables may be correlated, including the following:

- The two variables have a cause-and-effect relationship. That is, an increase in the value of one variable tends to cause an increase (or decrease) in the value of the other variable.

- The two variables have nothing directly to do with each other. However, an increase in the value of a third (lurking) variable tends to cause the values of each of the two variables to increase together, to decrease together, or one to increase and the other to decrease.

- Even though the correlation between the two variables is actually zero or close to zero, you get a non-zero correlation just by chance when you take a sample of values.

a Look back at Activity 2. Which situations seem to fit each category above?

b What type of directed graph best models each category above?

c How can you be certain whether a nonzero correlation coefficient means that there is a cause-and-effect relationship between two variables?

Be prepared to share your responses with the entire class.

MASTER 70

Understanding Pearson's Formula

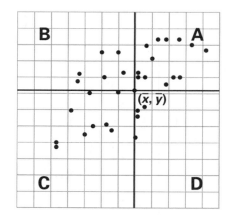

Region	Value of $(x - \bar{x})$	Value of $(y - \bar{y})$	Value of $(x - \bar{x})(y - \bar{y})$
A			
B			
C			
D			

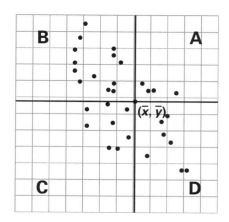

Think About This Situation

a The study reports a Pearson correlation coefficient of 0.927 for these data. Does that seem reasonable? Why?

b Your calculator or computer software can calculate the equation of a regression line. Try it with these data. What does the slope mean in the context of these data?

c The regression line you found in part b is called the *least squares* regression line. How do you think the idea of "least squares" might be used in finding this line?

d For which community does the regression line fit poorest?

Evaluating Functions

This "Technology Tip" will help you find the value of a function. You will need to enter the equation for the function into Y_1 and return to the home screen. The specific example shown below uses the linear regression equation to predict Arturo's ninth-grade GPA. (See page 213, Activity 1 part c.)

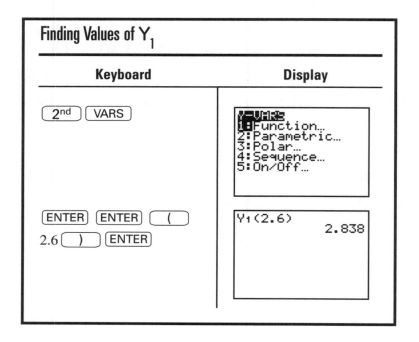

Evaluating Functions

This "Technology Tip" will help you find the value of a function. You will need to enter the equation for the function into Y_1 and return to the home screen. The specific example shown below uses the linear regression equation to predict Arturo's ninth-grade GPA. (See page 213, Activity 1 part c.)

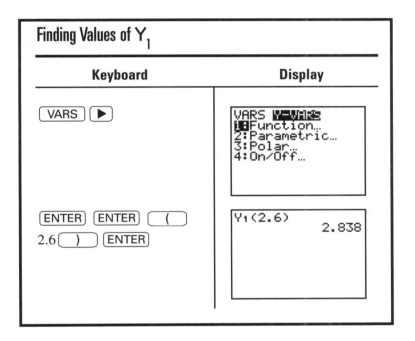

Checkpoint

ⓐ Describe two ways in which you can use a linear model to make a prediction.

ⓑ How can you find the difference between an observed value and the predicted value from the scatterplot? From the equation?

Be prepared to share your descriptions with the class.

Milwaukee School Statistics

School	% Attendance	Grade Point Average
Bay View	80	1.50
Custer	73	1.32
Hamilton	83	1.67
Juneau	84	1.77
King	92	2.30
Madison	73	1.60
Marshall	90	1.73
School of Arts	89	2.14
Milwaukee Tech	84	1.70
North Division	67	0.99
Pulaski	72	1.48
Riverside	86	2.06
South Division	74	1.43
Vincent	75	1.65
Washington	80	1.67

Source: *Milwaukee Journal*, January 23, 1994

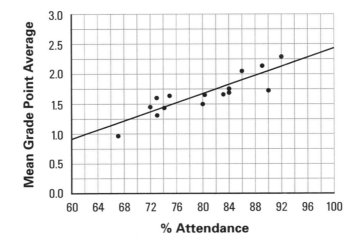

The "Best-Fitting" Line

x	y	Predicted y	Error	Squared Error
1	1			
2	2			
3	5			
		Total		

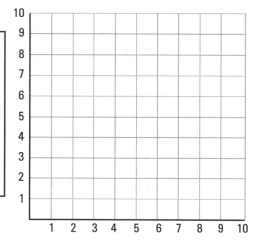

x	y	Predicted y	Error	Squared Error
1	1			
2	2			
3	5			
		Total		

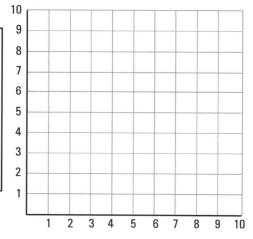

x	y	Predicted y	Error	Squared Error
1	1			
2	2			
3	5			
		Total		

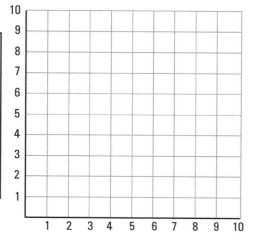

Checkpoint

a How is the idea of a sum of squared differences important to least squares regression?

b Describe two characteristics of the least squares regression line.

c Give an example to show that a low correlation doesn't always indicate that a line is not a good model for the data. Give an example to show that a high correlation doesn't always indicate that a line is a good model for the data.

Be prepared to discuss your group's responses with the entire class.

Crawling Age

Birth Month	Temperature (°F) at Age 6 Months	Age Began to Crawl (weeks)
January	66	29.84
February	73	30.52
March	72	29.70
April	63	31.84
May	52	28.58
June	39	31.44
July	33	33.64
August	30	32.82
September	33	33.83
October	37	33.35
November	48	33.38
December	57	32.32

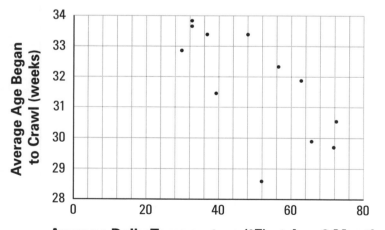

Checkpoint

a Describe how the idea of a sum of squared differences is used in correlation coefficients and in regression equations.

b Does a strong correlation imply a cause-and-effect relationship?

c How are regression lines used?

d Refer back to the "Think About This Situation" on page 171. How would you answer those questions now?

Be prepared to discuss your responses with the entire class.

1. The following table gives the birth rates per 1,000 people living in the United States for certain years.

Year	Birth Rate	Year	Birth Rate
1910	30.1	1955	25.0
1915	29.5	1960	23.7
1920	27.7	1965	19.4
1925	25.1	1970	18.4
1930	21.3	1975	14.8
1935	18.7	1980	15.9
1940	19.4	1985	15.8
1945	20.4	1990	16.7
1950	24.1		

Source: *Information Please Almanac*, 1993. Boston: Houghton Mifflin Company, 1992.

   a. Produce a scatterplot of the data. Discuss why it might be useful to model this data with a line. Why might one not want to model it with a line?

   b. Historically, what might explain the rates for the 1930s and 1950s?

   c. Predict the 1995 birth rate from the scatterplot.

   d. Find the linear regression equation for this data and graph it on your scatterplot. Then predict the 1995 birth rate using the linear regression line.

   e. Find the 1995 birth rate as reported by a current edition of the *Information Please Almanac*. Which of your predictions is closer to the actual birth rate?

   f. Report the correlation coefficient for this data. Why should you not use the correlation coefficient as your only criterion for deciding whether the linear regression line is a good model for a set of data?

2. Solve each system of equations by reasoning with the symbolic forms themselves. Check your solution. If you made an error in your reasoning, determine where your error occurred. Then explain how you could minimize the chance of repeating the same error when using symbolic reasoning to solve systems of equations.

   a. $3x + 2y = 5$
   $-2x + y = -1$

   b. $3x + 4y = 4.5$
   $x - 3y = -5$

   c. $y = 4$
   $y = 3 + 5x$

   d. $y = -3 + 2x$
   $3y = 3 + 6x$

3. Find an equation of the line satisfying the given conditions.

  a. With slope −3 and containing the point (3, −2)

  b. Containing the points (−3, 4) and (1, 2)

4. Make a sketch and then find the volume of each of the following space shapes.

  a. A square prism with 6 cm edges on bases and 12 cm height

  b. A triangular prism with a 10 cm height and a base with right angle sides of 6 cm and 5 cm

  c. A cylinder with a diameter of 10 cm and height of 6 cm

5. Find the solution to each equation by reasoning with the symbolic form itself. Check your solution by substitution. If you made an error in your symbolic reasoning, determine where your error occurred. Then explain how you can minimize the chance of repeating the same error when using symbolic reasoning to solve other similar equations.

  a. $1.5x + 3 = 6$ **b.** $2x + 3 = 4 - 2x$

  c. $2(3x - 5) = 8$ **d.** $3(2x - 3) + 4 = -4x + 8$

6. Here are three matrices.

$$A = \begin{bmatrix} 3 & -2 \\ 5 & 1 \end{bmatrix} \qquad B = \begin{bmatrix} 2 & 5 & 4 \\ 1 & 3 & 0 \end{bmatrix} \qquad C = \begin{bmatrix} 0 & -1 \\ 1 & 0 \end{bmatrix}$$

  a. Which two of the matrices may be added? Find the sum.

  b. Find a pair of matrices for which multiplication is possible in one order but not the other. Find the product.

  c. Which matrix could represent a triangle? Explain how it can represent a triangle.

  d. Which matrix could represent a rigid transformation? Use it to transform the triangle in part c.

Suggested Solutions

1. a. A line could be used to summarize the trend in this data, since the data seems to be decreasing and data points would be both above and below the line. A line might not be the best model since there seem to be regular fluctuations in the display. A line plot (plot over time) might be better for predicting between two adjacent data points. Also, one always must be careful when predicting too far into the future using a regression line.

b. The early 1930s was a time of great economic depression, which might help to explain the low birth rate. The 1950s was the decade following World War II, when soldiers returned home and many new families began. It was also a prosperous time for our nation, which may have influenced decisions on family size.

c. Using the scatterplot alone for predicting, student responses will vary but should be around 16.7.

d. The linear regression line for this data set (using $x = 10$ for 1910 *etc.* and rounding to the nearest hundredth) is $y = -0.16x + 29.41$.

Using the regression line to predict 1995 birth rates gives a birth rate of 14.21.

e. The 1995 reported birth rate per 1,000 people is 14.8. The linear regression equation gave a close prediction in this case, but this should not be generalized by students to all cases.

f. The correlation coefficient is approximately -0.825. When deciding whether a line is a good model for a set of data, one must carefully consider the context to see if it is reasonable to assume a linear trend, particularly for prediction beyond the data set. One must examine the graph for clusters or trends within the data set which might indicate a different model even though the correlation is high. Influential points must be checked for validity and carefully considered before being eliminated. Influential points can exert a weighted influence by either increasing or decreasing the correlation coefficient.

2. a. $x = 1$
$y = 1$

b. $x = -0.5$
$y = 1.5$

c. $x = \frac{1}{5}$
$y = 4$

d. No solution

3. a. $y = 7 - 3x$

b. $y = -\frac{1}{2}x + \frac{5}{2}$ or $x + 2y = 5$

Suggested Solutions (*continued*)

4. a.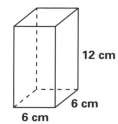

12 cm

6 cm

6 cm

$V = 36 \cdot 12 = 432$ cm^3

b.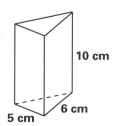

10 cm

6 cm

5 cm

The area of the base is $6 \cdot 5 \cdot \frac{1}{2}$ or 15 cm^2.
So the volume is $10 \cdot 15$ or 150 cm^3.

c.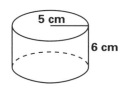

5 cm

6 cm

Base area is $\pi \cdot 5^2$.
Volume is $6 \cdot 5^2 \cdot \pi$ or 150π cm^3, which is approximately 471.24 cm^3.

5. a. $x = 2$ **b.** $x = \frac{1}{4}$

    c. $x = 3$ **d.** $x = 1.3$

6. a. Matricies A and C can be added together. $A + C = \begin{bmatrix} 3 & -3 \\ 6 & 1 \end{bmatrix}$

    b. There are 2 pairs, A and B or C and B.

$$A \cdot B = \begin{bmatrix} 3 & -2 \\ 5 & 1 \end{bmatrix} \cdot \begin{bmatrix} 2 & 5 & 4 \\ 1 & 3 & 0 \end{bmatrix} = \begin{bmatrix} 4 & 9 & 12 \\ 11 & 28 & 20 \end{bmatrix} \text{ or}$$

$$C \cdot B = \begin{bmatrix} 0 & -1 \\ 1 & 0 \end{bmatrix} \cdot \begin{bmatrix} 2 & 5 & 4 \\ 1 & 3 & 0 \end{bmatrix} = \begin{bmatrix} -1 & -3 & 0 \\ 2 & 5 & 4 \end{bmatrix}$$

    c. B could represent a triangle. The columns would be thought of as the *x*- and *y*-coordinates of the vertices of the triangle.

    d. Matrix C represents a 90° counterclockwise rotation.

$$C \cdot B = \begin{bmatrix} -1 & -3 & 0 \\ 2 & 5 & 4 \end{bmatrix}$$

Think About This Situation

When a new balloon is designed, the first step is to make a scale model that is smaller than the real balloon will be. Suppose that for a Big Bird balloon, a scale model is made that is $\frac{1}{20}$ of the planned full size.

a If the model is 2 feet tall, how tall would the full-size balloon be?

b If the model has a belt that is 1.5 feet around Big Bird's waist, how long would the belt be on the full-size balloon?

c If the model has a surface area of 6 square feet, how many square feet of material would be required to make the large balloon?

d If the model holds 2.5 cubic feet of air, what would the volume of the full-size balloon be?

e How would your answers to parts a–d change if the full-size balloon were to be only 10 times the size of the scale model?

Exploring Direct Variation Power Models

Edge Length (in units)	Perimeter of One Face (in units)	Area of One Face (in square units)	Total Surface Area of Cube (in square units)
1			
2			
3			
4			
5			
6			
7			
8			

Edge Length (in units)	Volume of Cube (in cubic units)
1	
2	
3	
4	
5	
6	
7	
8	

Checkpoint

Suppose that you measure the edge lengths of a collection of cubes of several different sizes and calculate the perimeter of a face, surface areas, and volumes.

 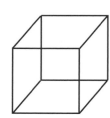 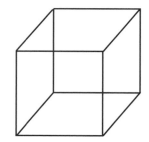

a Describe patterns in the tables, graphs, and symbolic rules that relate *edge length* to the following.

■ The perimeters of each face of the cubes

■ The areas of each face of the cubes

■ The total surface areas of the cubes

■ The volumes of the cubes

b What do these patterns suggest about the ways that measurements like lengths, areas, and volumes of any scale-model shape will be related to those same measurements on the full-size object?

Be prepared to share your pattern descriptions and thinking with the class.

Describing Graphs 1

Graph	Words or Phrases that Describe Patterns
$y = a + bx$	
$y = ax^2,\ a < 0$	

Describing Graphs II

Graph	Words or Phrases that describe Patterns
$y = a(b^x)$, $a > 0$ and $0 < b < 1$	
$y = ax^3$	

Checkpoint

Look back over your discoveries in the experiments with various power models.

a What patterns do you expect to find in tables and graphs of relations with equations of the form $y = ax^2$ when a is some positive number? When a is some negative number?

b What patterns do you expect to find in tables and graphs of relations with equations of the form $y = ax^3$ when a is some positive number? When a is some negative number?

c What patterns do you expect to find in tables and graphs of power models $y = x^n$ when n is a positive even integer? When n is a positive odd integer?

d How are the patterns in tables and graphs of power models different from those of linear and exponential models?

Be prepared to share your group's conclusions with the entire class.

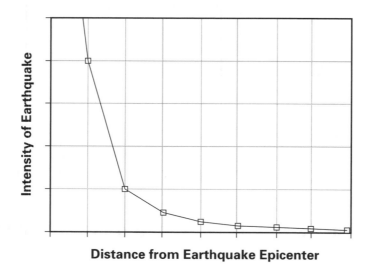

Intensity of Earthquake

Distance from Earthquake Epicenter

Think About This Situation

a How would you describe the pattern of change in earthquake intensity as distance from the epicenter increases?

b How well do you think each of the following suggestions will model the pattern relating distance and earthquake intensity?

- $y = a + bx$ with a positive and b negative.

- $y = a(b^x)$ with a large and b positive, but less than 1.

- $y = \dfrac{a}{x^2}$ with a positive.

Checkpoint

a What equation will relate distance d, average speed s, and driving time t for a trip?

b How does an increase in average speed change the expected driving time for a fixed distance?

c How is your answer to part b shown in graphs of (*speed, time*) relations for any fixed distance?

d How is your answer to part b related to the form of speed-time modeling equations for any fixed distance?

Be prepared to share your equation and interpretations with the class.

Exploring Light Intensity

Distance from Light (*D*)	1	2	3	4	5
Diameter of Light Circle (*d*)	2	4	6	8	10
Radius of Light Circle (*r*)					

Distance from Light (*D*)	1	2	3	4	5
Area of Light Circle (*A*)					

Distance from Light (*D*)	1	2	3	4	5
Area of Light Circle (*A*)	$\pi \approx 3.14$	$4\pi \approx 12.56$			
Light Intensity (*I*)	$\frac{160}{\pi} \approx 50.93$	$\frac{160}{4\pi} \approx 12.73$			

Checkpoint

a Suppose you aim a flashlight against one wall of a darkened room and gradually move the light away from the wall. What patterns of change would you expect

■ in the diameter of the light circle as a function of distance from the wall?

■ in the area of the light circle as a function of distance from the wall?

b Now suppose you also use a light meter to measure the intensity of light when the flashlight is at various distances from the wall. What pattern of results would you expect

■ in a table of (*distance, intensity*) data?

■ in a graph of the (*distance, intensity*) data?

c How are the patterns in part b related to the form of an algebraic rule expressing intensity *I* as a function of distance *D*?

Be prepared to share and justify your pattern descriptions.

Describing Graphs III

Graph	Words or Phrases that Describe Patterns
$y = \frac{a}{x}, a < 0$ 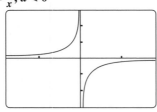	
$y = \frac{a}{x^2}, a > 0$ 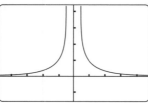	

Checkpoint

a Given below are rules and graphs of four inverse power models. The scales are the same on each graph. Match each graph with the rule it fits best and explain your reasoning.

i. $y = \frac{1}{x^2}$ **ii.** $y = \frac{2}{x}$ **iii.** $y = \frac{1}{x}$ **iv.** $y = \frac{0.2}{x^2}$

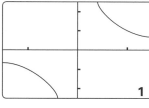
1

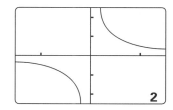
2

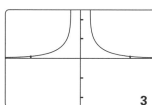
3

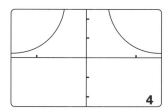
4

b What patterns can be expected in tables of (x, y) values for each rule?

c What patterns of symmetry appear in graphs of the basic types of inverse power models $y = \frac{1}{x}$ and $y = \frac{1}{x^2}$?

Be prepared to share your group's conclusions with the entire class.

Think About This Situation

a What sort of graph would you expect for the (*time in flight, height*) relation?

b How could you use the given rule relating height to time in flight to find when the shot might reach the height of the basket (10 feet)?

c If the shot misses the basket without hitting anything else, when will it hit the floor?

Checkpoint

The problems about platform divers and football punts involved models that were similar to, but a bit different from, the familiar power models. Compare the diving and punting models to the power model $y = 4.9x^2$.

a How is the graph of $y = 10 - 4.9x^2$ similar to and different from the graph of $y = 4.9x^2$ or $y = -4.9x^2$?

b How is the graph of $y = -4.9x^2 + 4x + 3$ similar to and different from the graph of $y = 4.9x^2$ or $y = -4.9x^2$?

c How are the patterns in tables for $y = 10 - 4.9x^2$ and $y = -4.9x^2 + 4x + 3$ similar to and different from those for the power models $y = 4.9x^2$ or $y = -4.9x^2$?

d How could you predict the patterns in tables and graphs by looking at the ways the symbolic rules for the new relations are built from the basic rule $y = 4.9x^2$?

Be prepared to share your observations and thinking with the class.

Checkpoint

ⓐ What is the shape of the graph giving profit as a function of concert ticket price? What does that graph tell you about the relation between those variables?

ⓑ How would the pattern in the profit graph be displayed in a table of (*ticket price, profit*) values for ticket prices from $1 to $15?

ⓒ Where are break-even and maximum profit points on the graph? In the table?

Be prepared to explain your responses to the class.

Checkpoint

Describe the sort of graph and table patterns that can be expected for a quadratic model with rule in the form $y = ax^2 + bx + c$, in each case below. Then describe how the graph is related to the graph of the basic power model $y = x^2$.

a $y = ax^2$, $[b = 0, c = 0]$

b $y = x^2 + c$, $[a = 1, b = 0]$

c $y = ax^2 + c$, $[b = 0]$

d $y = x^2 + bx + c$, $[a = 1, b \neq 0]$

e $y = ax^2 + bx + c$, $[a \neq 0, b \neq 0]$

Be prepared to share your descriptions with the entire class.

Checkpoint

Suppose that in modeling some situation, you are required to solve a quadratic equation like

$$50 = 3.4x^2 + 4.5x + 23.5.$$

a What is the goal of the process?

b How can you use a table of values to find the solution or solutions?

c Describe two ways of using a graph to find the solution or solutions.

d How can the solution or solutions be checked without using a table or graph?

e How could you find the solution or solutions by reasoning with the symbolic form if there were no linear term $4.5x$?

Be prepared to explain your solution methods to the entire class.

Checkpoint

Think about the meaning and methods of solving a quadratic equation in the form $d = ax^2 + bx + c$.

a What are the possible numbers of solutions that can occur?

b How would you go about deciding how many solutions there actually are?

c How would you go about finding and checking the solutions?

Be prepared to share your methods for analyzing and solving a quadratic equation.

Think About This Situation

a Does the scaffolding pictured in the text appear to have enough cross-braces to ensure that it is rigid? Explain your reasoning.

b What geometric principle explains why scaffold cross-bracing works?

c How would you determine the length of cross-braces to use on a particular scaffold grid?

Checkpoint

Think about the patterns you discovered in this investigation as you answer the following questions.

a If r and s are two positive numbers, how can you check to see if $r = \sqrt{s}$?

b If b and h are the base and height of a rectangle, how can you calculate the length of a diagonal of that rectangle?

c If some calculation produces $\sqrt{n}$ as a result, how can you go about writing that result in simplest radical form? How can you check that the new form is actually equivalent to the original?

Be prepared to explain your calculations and checks to the entire class.

Drawing a Spiral

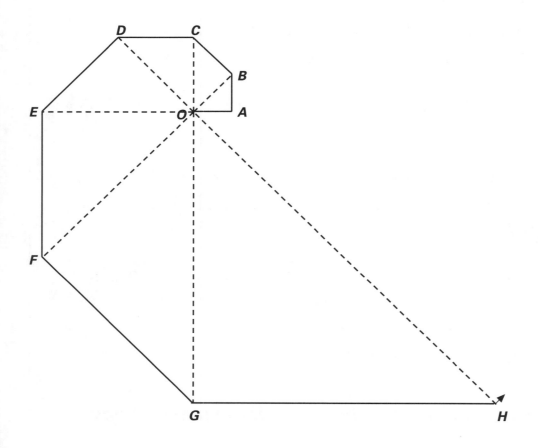

Checkpoint

Suppose that a spiral design begins as in the following figure.

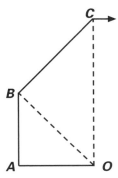

a If $\angle A$ is a right angle and $OA = AB$, what can you say about the other angles of $\triangle OAB$?

b How is the length of OB related to the length of OA and AB?

c If $\angle OBC$ is a right angle and $OB = BC$, what can you say about the other angles of $\triangle OBC$?

d How is the length of OC related to the length of OB and BC? How is the length of OC related to the length of OA and AB?

Be prepared to compare your responses with those of other groups.

Checkpoint

Radicals and exponential forms are also useful models of cubic relations, like those that occur in finding volumes of solid figures.

a What are the radical and exponential expressions for "the cube root of x"?

b How can you solve equations of the form $x^3 = a$ using a graph, a table of values, or a single arithmetic calculation?

c When you find a possible solution for the equation $x^3 = a$, how can you check it?

d How can you find the required edge length e for a cube that is to have some specified volume v?

Be prepared to explain your ideas to the entire class.

Checkpoint

Rewrite each of the following exponential expressions in an equivalent form. For each, also state the general rule that applies.

a $b^r \cdot b^s$

b $(m^a)^b$

c $\left(\dfrac{c}{r}\right)^a$

d $b^{\frac{1}{a}}$

e $\dfrac{t^r}{t^s}$

f $(ab)^n$

g a^{-b}

Be prepared to share your ideas with the rest of the class.

Checkpoint

In this unit you have investigated many situations where power and quadratic models are useful.

ⓐ What situations would you choose as good illustrations of the following?

- A direct variation power model

- An inverse variation power model

- A quadratic model

- A radical or fractional power model

ⓑ What patterns in graphs would you sketch in each case?

ⓒ What kinds of questions would you ask in each situation?

ⓓ For questions that call for solving quadratic equations,

- how would you find the solution?

- how would you check the solution?

- how many solutions would you expect, and how is that shown by graphs of quadratic relations?

Be prepared to share your examples and descriptions with the class.

Constructing a Math Toolkit
Concepts/Definitions/Relationships and Properties

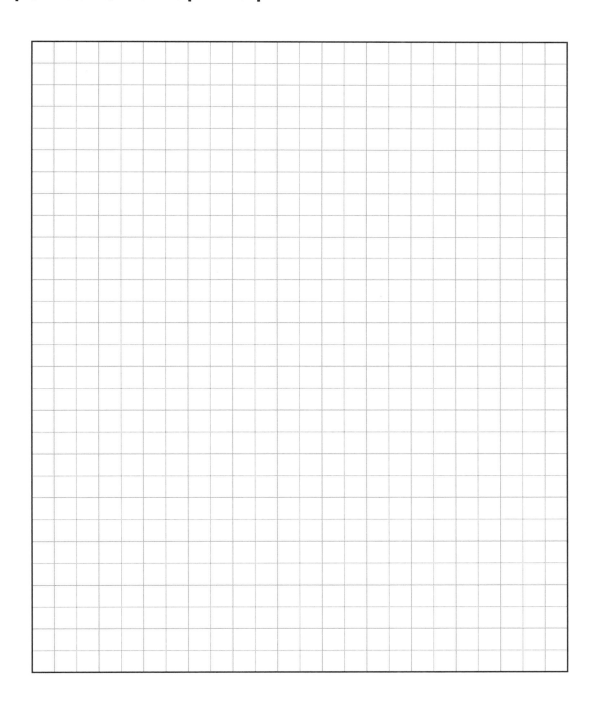

Constructing a Math Toolkit
Concepts/Definitions/Relationships and Properties

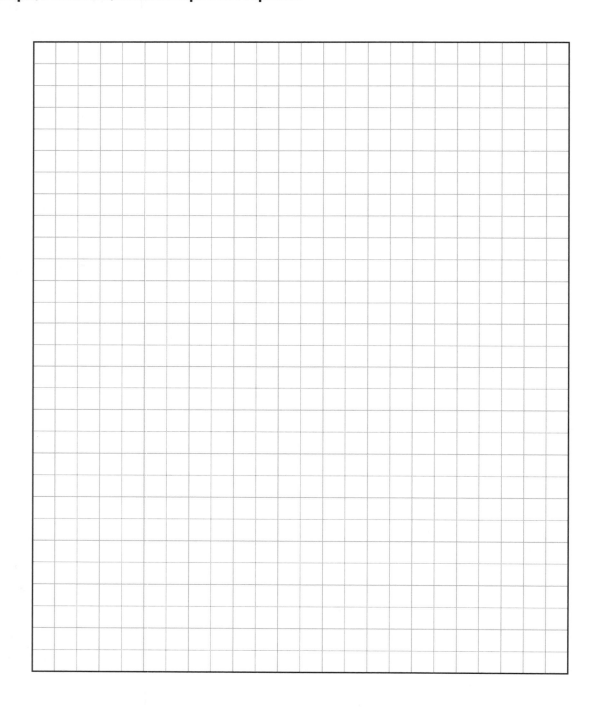

Constructing a Math Toolkit
Concepts/Definitions/Relationships and Properties

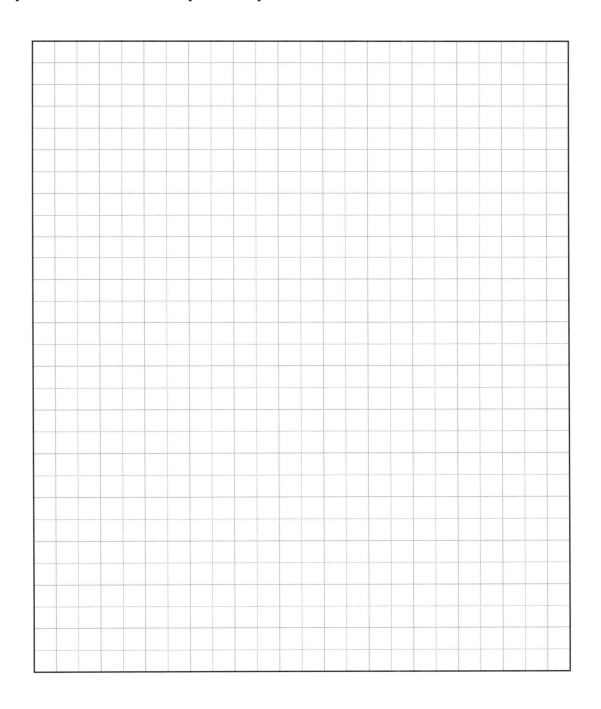

Constructing a Math Toolkit
Concepts/Definitions/Relationships and Properties

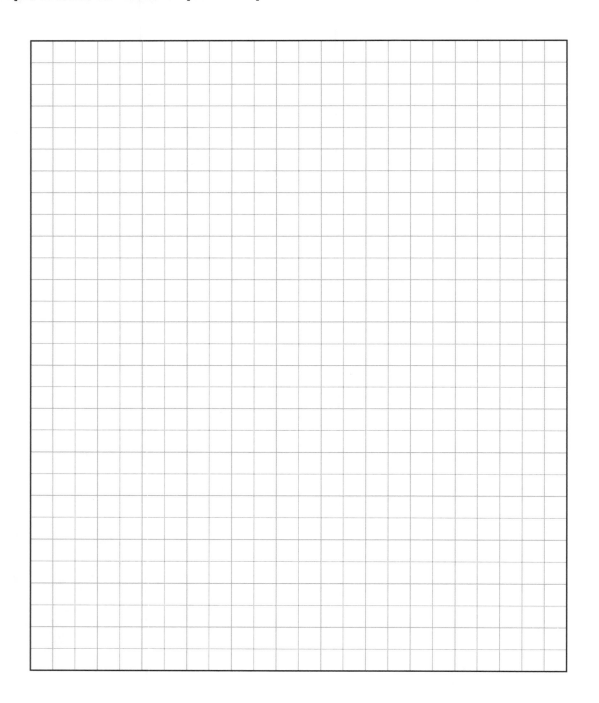

Constructing a Math Toolkit

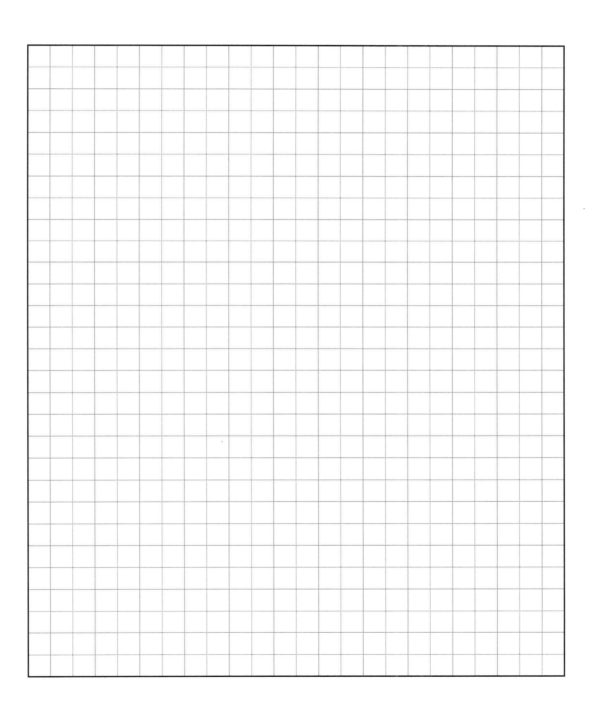

MASTER
111

Group Work

1. Discuss and decide responses to activities _____ on page(s) _____. Each group member must help to give ideas and opinions.

2. Random reporters will be selected for class discussion.

3. Questions will be accepted from groups only, and any member of the group may be called upon to ask the question.

   You have _____ min. to work

   (from _____:_____ to _____:_____).

**MASTER
112**

Evaluating My Group Work

	Yes	Somewhat	No
1. I participated in this investigation by contributing ideas.	_____	_____	_____
2. I was considerate of others, showed appreciation of ideas, and encouraged others to respond.	_____	_____	_____
3. I paraphrased others' responses and asked others to explain their thinking and work.	_____	_____	_____
4. I listened carefully and disagreed in an agreeable manner.	_____	_____	_____
5. I checked others' understanding of the work.	_____	_____	_____
6. I helped others in the group understand the solution(s) and strategies.	_____	_____	_____
7. We all agreed on the solution(s).	_____	_____	_____
8. I stayed on task and got the group back to work when necessary.	_____	_____	_____
9. We asked the teacher for assistance only if everyone in the group had the same question.	_____	_____	_____

10. What actions helped the group work productively?

11. What actions could make the group even more productive tomorrow?

Your signature: _____

Plots

———— , page ————

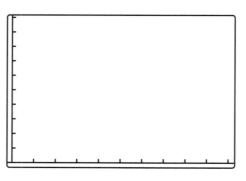

```
WINDOW
 Xmin= _____
 Xmax= _____
 Xscl= _____
 Ymin= _____
 Ymax= _____
 Yscl= _____
```

———— , page ————

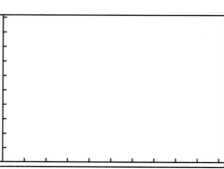

```
WINDOW
 Xmin= _____
 Xmax= _____
 Xscl= _____
 Ymin= _____
 Ymax= _____
 Yscl= _____
```

———— , page ————

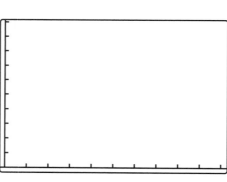

```
WINDOW
 Xmin= _____
 Xmax= _____
 Xscl= _____
 Ymin= _____
 Ymax= _____
 Yscl= _____
```

———— , page ————

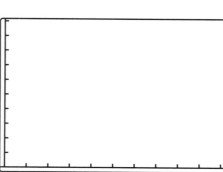

```
WINDOW
 Xmin= _____
 Xmax= _____
 Xscl= _____
 Ymin= _____
 Ymax= _____
 Yscl= _____
```

Graphs

———, page ———

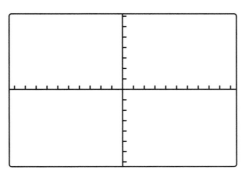

```
WINDOW
Xmin= _____
Xmax= _____
Xscl= _____
Ymin= _____
Ymax= _____
Yscl= _____
```

———, page ———

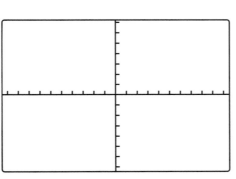

```
WINDOW
Xmin= _____
Xmax= _____
Xscl= _____
Ymin= _____
Ymax= _____
Yscl= _____
```

———, page ———

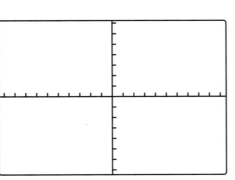

```
WINDOW
Xmin= _____
Xmax= _____
Xscl= _____
Ymin= _____
Ymax= _____
Yscl= _____
```

———, page ———

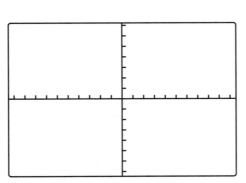

```
WINDOW
Xmin= _____
Xmax= _____
Xscl= _____
Ymin= _____
Ymax= _____
Yscl= _____
```

Y=
```
Y1=■
Y2=
Y3=
Y4=
Y5=
Y6=
Y7=
Y8=
```

STAT PLOT
```
STAT PLOTS
1:Plot1...
   Off  L1 L2 □
2:Plot2...
   Off  L1 L3 +
3:Plot3...
   Off  L1 L4 ·
4↓PlotsOff
```

WINDOW
```
WINDOW FORMAT
 Xmin=-10
 Xmax=10
 Xscl=1
 Ymin=-10
 Ymax=10
 Yscl=1
```

FORMAT
```
WINDOW FORMAT
RectGC  PolarGC
CoordOn CoordOff
GridOff GridOn
AxesOn  AxesOff
LabelOff LabelOn
```

TblSet
```
TABLE SETUP
 TblMin=1
 △Tbl=1
Indpnt: Auto Ask
Depend: Auto Ask
```

ZOOM
```
ZOOM MEMORY
1:ZBox
2:Zoom In
3:Zoom Out
4:ZDecimal
5:ZSquare
6:ZStandard
7↓ZTrig
```

MODE
```
Normal Sci Eng
Float 0123456789
Radian Degree
Func Par Pol Seq
Connected Dot
Sequential Simul
FullScreen Split
```

LINK
```
SEND RECEIVE
1:SelectAll+...
2:SelectAll-...
3:SelectCurrent...
4:Back Up...
```

RECEIVE
```
SEND RECEIVE
1:Receive
```

STAT
```
EDIT CALC
1:Edit...
2:SortA(
3:SortD(
4:ClrList
```

CALC
```
EDIT CALC
1:1-Var Stats
2:2-Var Stats
3:SetUp...
4:Med-Med
5:LinReg(ax+b)
6:QuadReg
7↓CubicReg
```

LIST
```
OPS MATH
1:SortA(
2:SortD(
3:dim
4:Fill(
5:seq(
```

MATH
```
OPS MATH
1:min(
2:max(
3:mean(
4:median(
5:sum
6:prod
```

MATH
```
MATH NUM HYP PRB
1:▶Frac
2:▶Dec
3:3
4:3√
5:×√
6:fMin(
7↓fMax(
```

NUM
```
MATH NUM CPX PRB
1:round(
2:iPart
3:fPart
4:int
5:min(
6:max(
```

PRB
```
MATH NUM HYP PRB
1:rand
2:nPr
3:nCr
4:!
```

PRGM
```
EXEC EDIT NEW
1:PERTPROG
```

MEM
```
MEMORY
1:Check RAM...
2:Delete...
3:Reset...
```

RESET
```
RESET MEMORY
1:No
2:Reset

Resetting memory
erases all data
and programs.
```

Y=

```
Plot1 Plot2 Plot3
\Y1=█
\Y2=
\Y3=
\Y4=
\Y5=
\Y6=
\Y7=
```

STAT PLOT

```
STAT PLOTS
1:Plot1…Off
    ░░ L1   1
2:Plot2…Off
    ∠ L1  L3   +
3:Plot3…Off
    ∠ L1  L2   □
4↓PlotsOff
```

PLOT 1

```
Plot1 Plot2 Plot3
On Off
Type: ∠ ∠ ░░
      ·□· ░ΔΔ ░░
Xlist:L1
Freq:1
```

PLOT 2

```
Plot1 Plot2 Plot3
On Off
Type: ∠ ∠ ░░
      ·□· ·□· ░░
Xlist:L1
Ylist:L3
Mark: □ + ·
```

WINDOW

```
WINDOW
 Xmin=-10
 Xmax=10
 Xscl=1
 Ymin=-10
 Ymax=10
 Yscl=1
 Xres=1
```

TBLSET

```
TABLE SETUP
 TblStart=1
 ΔTbl=.1
Indpnt: Auto Ask
Depend: Auto Ask
```

ZOOM

```
ZOOM MEMORY
1:ZBox
2:Zoom In
3:Zoom Out
4:ZDecimal
5:ZSquare
6:ZStandard
7↓ZTrig
```

ZOOM

```
ZOOM MEMORY
4↑ZDecimal
5:ZSquare
6:ZStandard
7:ZTrig
8:ZInteger
9:ZoomStat
0:ZoomFit
```

FORMAT

```
RectGC PolarGC
CoordOn CoordOff
GridOff GridOn
AxesOn AxesOff
LabelOff LabelOn
ExprOn ExprOff
```

MODE

```
Normal Sci Eng
Float 0123456789
Radian Degree
Func Par Pol Seq
Connected Dot
Sequential Simul
Real a+bi re^θi
Full Horiz G-T
```

LINK

```
SEND RECEIVE
1:All+…
2:All-…
3:Prgm…
4:List…
5:Lists to TI82…
6:GDB…
7↓Pic…
```

RECEIVE

```
SEND RECEIVE
1:Receive
```

STAT

```
EDIT CALC TESTS
1:Edit…
2:SortA(
3:SortD(
4:ClrList
5:SetUpEditor
```

CALC

```
EDIT CALC TESTS
1:1-Var Stats
2:2-Var Stats
3:Med-Med
4:LinReg(ax+b)
5:QuadReg
6:CubicReg
7↓QuartReg
```

LIST OPS

```
NAMES OPS MATH
1:SortA(
2:SortD(
3:dim(
4:Fill(
5:seq(
6:cumSum(
7↓ΔList(
```

LIST MATH

```
NAMES OPS MATH
1:min(
2:max(
3:mean(
4:median(
5:sum(
6:prod(
7↓stdDev(
```

MATH

```
MATH NUM CPX PRB
1:▶Frac
2:▶Dec
3:³
4:³√(
5:ˣ√
6:fMin(
7↓fMax(
```

NUM

```
MATH NUM CPX PRB
1:abs(
2:round(
3:iPart(
4:fPart(
5:int(
6:min(
7↓max(
```

PRB

```
MATH NUM CPX PRB
1:rand
2:nPr
3:nCr
4:!
5:randInt(
6:randNorm(
7:randBin(
```

TEST

```
TEST LOGIC
1:=
2:≠
3:>
4:≥
5:<
6:≤
```

PRGM

```
EXEC EDIT NEW
1:PERTPROG
```

VARS

```
VARS Y-VARS
1:Window…
2:Zoom…
3:GDB…
4:Picture…
5:Statistics…
6:Table…
7:String…
```

Y-VARS

```
VARS Y-VARS
1:Function…
2:Parametric…
3:Polar…
4:On/Off…
```

MEM

```
MEMORY
1:Check RAM…
2:Delete…
3:Clear Entries
4:ClrAllLists
5:Reset…
```